INGENIOUS

PRODUCT DESIGN THAT WORKS

promopress

Edited by Wang Shaoqiang

INGENIOUS

PRODUCT DESIGN THAT WORKS

Editor: Wang Shaoqiang
English preface revised by: Tom Corkett

PROMOPRESS is a brand of:
Promotora de Prensa Internacional S.A.
C/ Ausiàs March, 124
08013 Barcelona, Spain
Phone: 0034 93 245 14 64
Fax: 0034 93 265 48 83
info@promopress.es
www.promopresseditions.com
Facebook: Promopress Editions
Twitter: Promopress Editions @PromopressEd

Sponsored by Design 360°
– Concept and Design Magazine
Edited and produced by
Sandu Publishing Co., Ltd.
Book design, concepts & art direction by
Sandu Publishing Co., Ltd.
info@sandupublishing.com

Cover design: Dingding Huo

ISBN: 978-84-16851-32-4
D.L.: B-23146-2017

Printed in China

CONTENTS

Preface   *006*

● FURNITURE

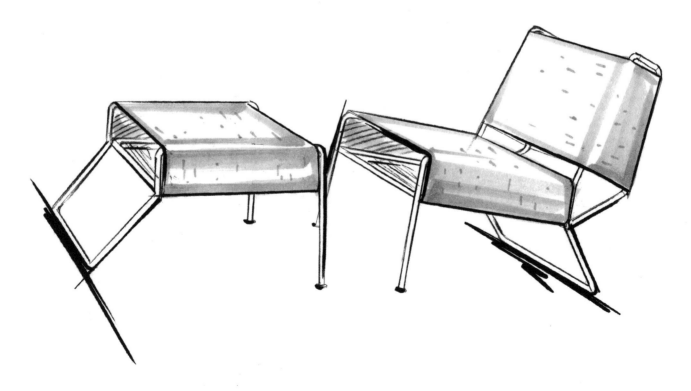

●● LIGHTING

●●● ACCESSORIES

PREFACE

Interactions Between Humans and Objects

By Juno Jeon

Ever since human beings invented the first tool, we have been amassing more and more objects. The first objects that we owned such as clothes or weapons were always related to our survival. As time moved on, our ancestors settled down to farm, and we started to own things such as houses, livestock, land and so on to meet our demands for a better life. The wheel of possession has rolled over and over through the years, and nowadays we cannot imagine a life without products at hand. The fact is that now that we no longer live naked in nature, products can be found anytime and everywhere in our daily lives.

Even though we have been living with products throughout human history, the history of product design spans merely one century. Of course, some people may argue that we started to design products right at the moment when we invented the first tools. But "product design" as a conscious practice dates back to when we started to regard "product designer" as an occupation during the modern industrialized era. Since this period began, product designers have been trying to create and manufacture products suited in various ways to our modes of living.

Some product designers try to make financially efficient products that can generate more profit for a company. They aspire to develop a better production system or center out of materials that can reduce production costs while improving quality. Others try to come up with products that bring about better user experiences for customers. They develop better shapes or interfaces that enable products to be used more comfortably. And still others try to make aesthetically pleasing products that attract people's attentions and convince them to buy the product. Visually pleasing products can give satisfaction to users and enliven the spaces in which they spend their time.

Although many different strands of product design have developed, they all have an essential common element: interaction between human and object. Products cannot bear any meaning if they do not involve interaction with people. In other words, if we do not interact with products but merely put them in the corner of our room, they are literally nothing. Beautiful or luxurious product design interacts with us by giving us emotional satisfaction. Sometimes these products do not physically interact with us, yet they still make a difference to users or their living environment. Moreover, if there is no human involvement, there can be no such thing as "beauty" or "luxury." Functional or comfortable product design interacts with us by offering us a better user experience. In this case, products offer us physical satisfaction. But we should be aware that if human beings have different body shapes, so-called comfortable or functional design would take a completely different form to what we have become used to. In other words, the external features of a product depend on how human beings look and feel. In a word, we interact and communicate with products, either physically or emotionally, and there is a reciprocal influence between products and people. This is what I believe is the essence of product design.

In modern life, we tend not to sense products around us because they have been part of our daily lives for such a long time. We do not recognize our interactions with them when they do not trigger anything new. This seems kind of sad to me, because there are a lot of possibilities for making our routines better and more interesting with creative and lively products. Products are not just objects; they actually live together with us. When we were children, we used to give names to all of our belongings and interact with them. However, as we grow up, we start to forget the connection— products become lifeless objects. In my view, I think that designers should use their originality to revive the interaction between us and objects, and I believe that this is the new role that product designers should embrace.

You will see many bold examples of product design in the following pages of this volume. These products interact with users in various ways that are not limited to those mentioned above, and they have the power to inspire new thoughts and ideas.

Juno Jeon is a Korean-born furniture designer based in the Netherlands. He brings seemingly ordinary objects to life with his unique designs. His work centers on interactions between objects and people. He has received the New Talent award at the DMY International Design Festival in 2016.

www.junojunos.com

FURNITURE

From tables and chairs to ingenious storage solutions—this chapter brings to you inspiring visuals of stylish and well-tailored furniture designs, which perfectly fit contemporary homes, offices, and specific spaces.

Kollar

DESIGN /
Virosh Rangalla

Inspired by wood joinery and mechanical puzzles, Kollar is a fastener-less stool designed for the urban, contemporary environment. The inception of the concept came from three initial design criteria—the stool should exhibit simple and costeffective manufacturing, it should require no tools to assemble, and should have storage ability. Ideation revolved around the way in which pieces can interlock to create rigidity and structure, while maintaining a minimal, contemporary aesthetic. This inspired the idea of using two symmetrical leg components to create a collar to fit a seat assembly, hence the designer chose to name the stool "Kollar."

MATERIAL

Different materials are used for different components. The legs are made from recycled polypropylene. The seat assembly consists of three pieces of birch wood fastened together. Rare earth magnets are glued into the legs and stainless steel pucks are glued to the underside of the seat.

CREATIVE

The legs are manufactured using rotational molding to meet the stool's light weight, rigidity, and consistent wall thickness. The manufacturing process emphasizes its simplicity and cost-effective nature.

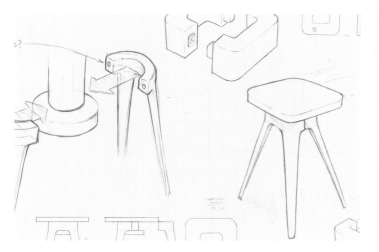

KOLLAR

MAKING

The seat is cut to shape and can be screwed together by hand. The legs can be disassembled or interlocked easily without the use of any tools.

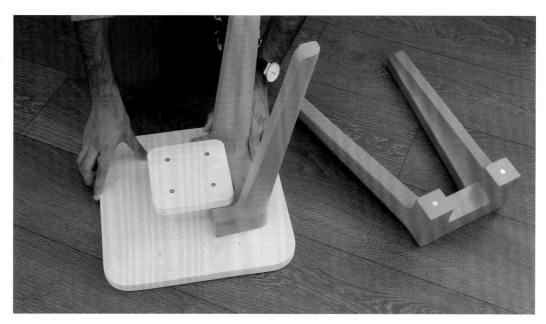

MARCO Bench & Stool

AGENCY /
Dragos Motica Studio

CLIENT /
Ubikubi

Marco is a strong visual trademark of its family range. Light yet strong, Marco Bench is a versatile seating solution. Versatile, simple and modern, it features a very comfortable seat with gently bounded edges, crafted from natural cork. Smart and playful, Marco Stool is a lightweight and easy to handle stool. It does not take up much space and can be used in many different ways, both in residential and public spaces.

CREATIVE

Both the bench and stool work perfectly as a seating alongside residential kitchen and restaurant tables, but also as an addition to hallways, bathrooms, and bedrooms, as well as a beautiful yet practical touch in commercial and outdoor environments.

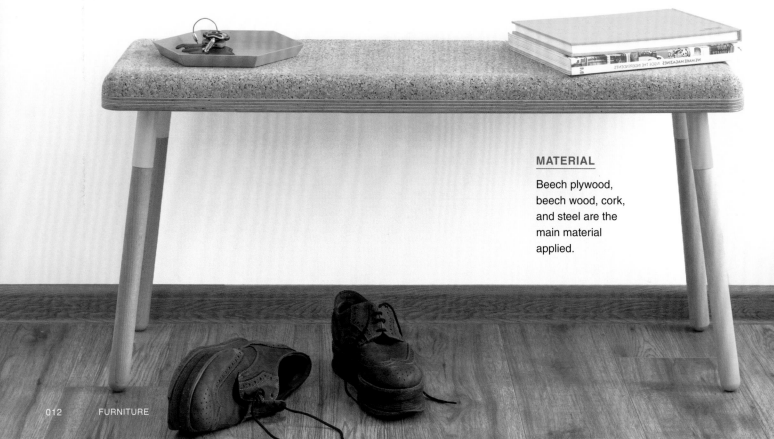

MATERIAL

Beech plywood, beech wood, cork, and steel are the main material applied.

MAKING

The bench and stool are built upon solid turned legs, with cylindrical metal joint reinforcements lacquered in various shades. Outstanding materials make them very durable and easy to clean.

Zero Per Stool

AGENCY /
HATTERN

Zero Per Stool is consisted of two parts which are the legs with white oak wood and the upper board with application of hybrid wood technique. The offcuts from the legs are solidified with cured resin and transformed to the upper board as the seat of the stool. By this, the waste produced from the product is reduced to almost zero. The interesting shape of woods and various colored combinations of the translucent resin present new aesthetic beauty to the consumers.

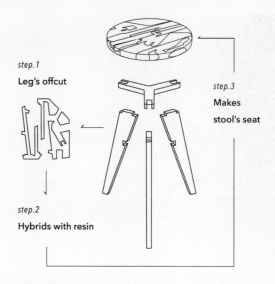

step.1

Leg's offcut

step.3

Makes stool's seat

step.2

Hybrids with resin

MATERIAL

Wood and resin are the main material.

MAKING

Hybrid wood technique is used to solidify cured resin with cracked wood pieces being poured into a mold. The translucent resin is to exhibit the shape of abandoned woods.

CREATIVE

Excessive efficiency-oriented manufacturing method inevitably causes massive waste. This project is an alternative to such manufacture concept, which has sought for "how to make a chair" in a new way.

Hangzhou Stool

AGENCY /
Chen Min Office

DESIGN /
Chen Min

PHOTOGRAPHY /
Zhang Sheng

The Hangzhou Stool consists of 16 layers of bamboo veneer, measuring 0.9mm in thickness. Every piece of the 16 bamboo veneers is different in length. The veneers are bent into an arc shape and glued together at each end, like the ripples on the water surface. The more weight the stool receives, the deeper the arc, providing more elasticity for the user. There is one piece of raw bamboo stick that penetrates the veneers, combining the two ends of the stool.

MATERIAL

Bamboo veneer and glue are used for making the stool.

CREATIVE

The designer uses extra thin bamboo veneer to give the stool a great beauty and elasticity.

MAKING

Several ultra thin bamboo layers are aligned vertical to each other adhering to the natural habits of bamboo fibers. In this way, each veneer becomes less flexible but more robust in all directions.

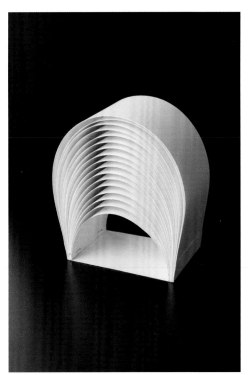
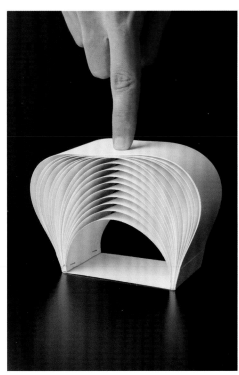

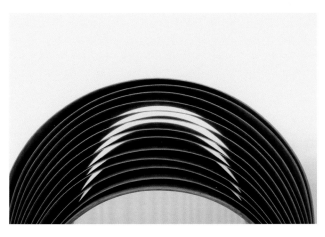

L01-Chair

AGENCY /
Line Design Studio

DESIGN /
Alexandr Vezlomtsev

PHOTOGRAPHY /
Vitaliy Fandorin

L01-Chair is an attempt to see an everyday item from a new perspective. The main idea of L01-Chair is simplicity and graphicness. Lines are diluted with warm shades of living wood. The designers decided to revise the design of an ordinary chair thereby to come up with something more simple and light. When the sketches were developed, they came across a complicated situation of choosing the right materials that would endure the maximum strength of the structure. In the end their choice fell on a kind of thin-walled steel pipe, 22mm in diameter, noted for its strength and tenacity. They put together the whole structure with an ash wood shield, 30mm in thickness. L01-Chair is the first item of Line Design Studio's furniture collection L0 line, which has established a stylistic direction for the upcoming products of L0 line.

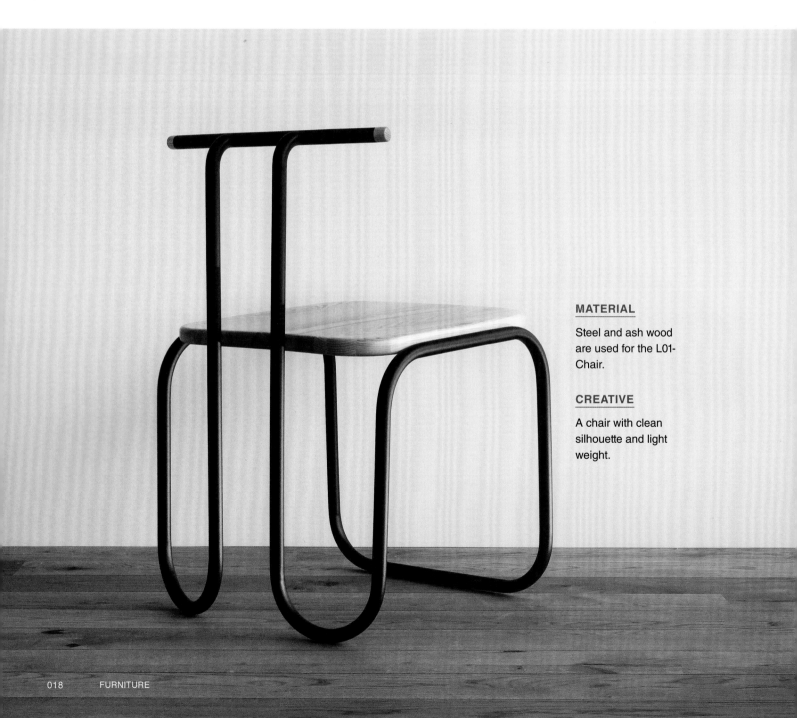

MATERIAL

Steel and ash wood are used for the L01-Chair.

CREATIVE

A chair with clean silhouette and light weight.

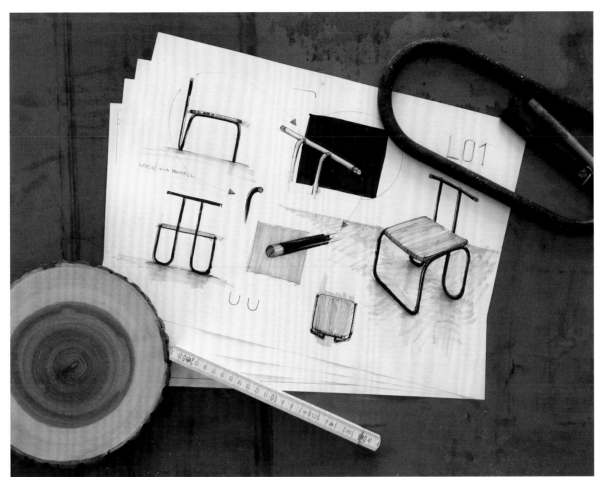

MAKING

L01-Chair was made and put together mainly by hand. The bending process of the steel pipe was performed on a machine that was made specifically for L01-Chair. The process of welding, polishing, and preparing wooden details were all performed manually.

Stol

DESIGN /
Kaleb Cárdenas

"Stol" means "chair" in Swedish. Kaleb Cárdenas designed this chair at Carl Malmsten Furniture Studies in Stockholm, Sweden. Originated from Mexico, Kaleb desired to build his first chair in Sweden in homage to the great furniture culture of this country. But it was also his desire to take this chair with him when he returned to Mexico. This was one of the reasons that he came up with "Stol," which can be easily disassembled and packaged.

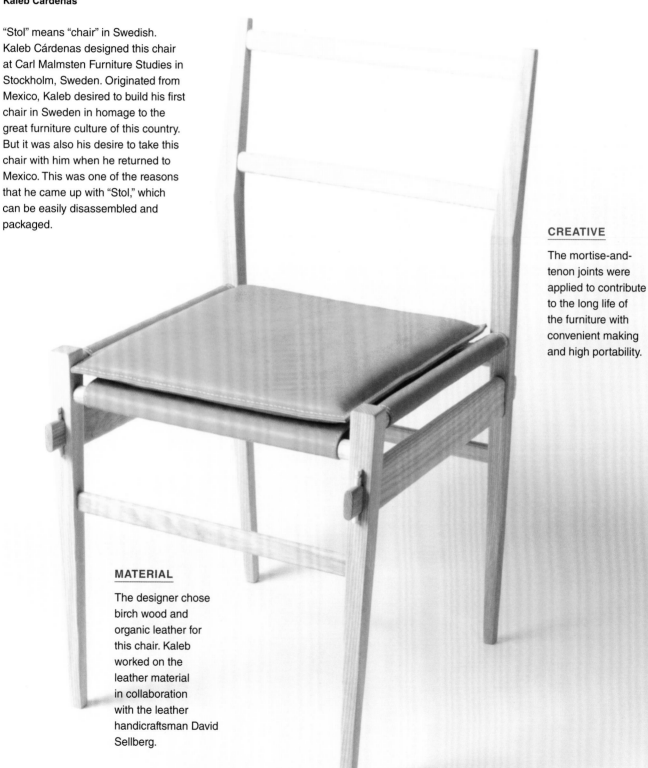

CREATIVE

The mortise-and-tenon joints were applied to contribute to the long life of the furniture with convenient making and high portability.

MATERIAL

The designer chose birch wood and organic leather for this chair. Kaleb worked on the leather material in collaboration with the leather handicraftsman David Sellberg.

MAKING

No fasteners were needed. The chair was mainly of mortise and tenon joints. The cross-rail tenons were pierced and protruded beyond the mortise. The through-tenons were further secured with wood keys driven vertically through the protruding end of the tenon. When the tenons were pulled out, the chair could be folded up.

Accordion Stool

AGENCY /
Dackelid-Form

DESIGN /
Nathalie Dackelid

FABRIC SPONSOR /
Gabriel.dk

PHOTOGRAPHY /
Clémence Lamm, Nathalie Dackelid

There is a popular saying in Sweden: If there is room in the heart there is space. This roughly means that there is always space for another person. Therefore, the designer created a functional furniture that can be extended based on user's individual needs. After doing loads of research on traditional craft techniques of extending surfaces, the designer succeeded in creating a stool that could be extended to almost double its original length, by using dove tail rails and a couple of leather straps together with the triangular batons. With this stool, users can make room for more guests whenever the situation requires. The stool was 460mm in length, with the maximum extended length of 820mm, 350mm in width, and 460mm in height.

CREATIVE

An expandable stool with clean shape and practical function.

MATERIAL

The stool was made of Swedish ash wood with the beautiful features and color range. The natural tanned leather was made from scraps. The whole stool was put together with brass screws. The designer used a transparent Osmo Oil as a finish for the furniture. The fabric on the seat was made out of wool from New Zealand.

MAKING

This project was about finding a solution to compact furniture in a neat way. The process was mostly about working with the material and finding the answer within the wood itself. The designer spent a period of intensive research and practice in the workshop, testing many different solutions of how a stool could be made into a bench.

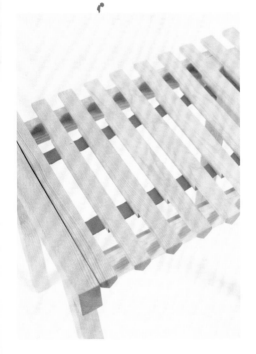

DUNE

DESIGN /
Lisa Ertel

PHOTOGRAPHY /
Michelle Mantel

Dune is a family of seating furniture made of solid wood. It is the result of observing how time forms material. The designer has applied sandblasting technique to imitate the force of nature—the soft early wood has been removed with artificial "growth rings" left on the wood surface. The dynamic structure created by the interplay of light and shadow makes nature and the individual history of the wood visible and tangible. The archaic form is inspired by stone benches called "Ruhstein." These contemporary witnesses were built in the area around south Germany and France in the 16th century.

MATERIAL

The designer chose spruce wood as the material.

CREATIVE

There can be varied combinations of the wood bricks.

MAKING

Sandblaster is used to create the unique texture of the wood, which indicates the passage of the time and life.

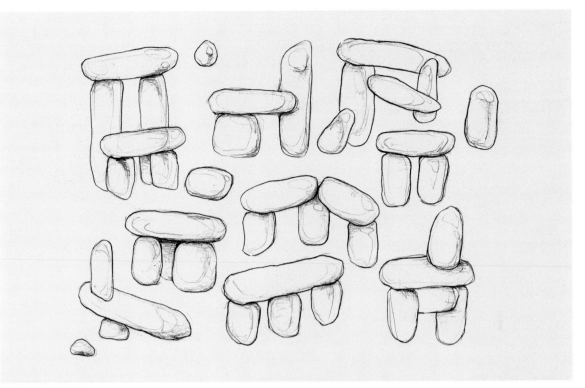

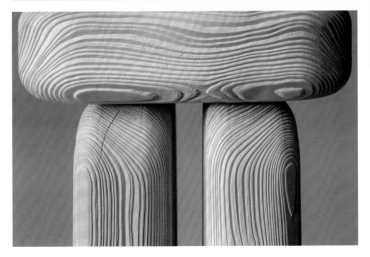

Peeking Chair

DESIGN /
Juno Jeon

PHOTOGRAPHY /
Juno Jeon

The designer wanted to create something to protect his privacy but at the same time allow some room for communication with others. This was how the idea of "Peeking chair" came into being. Instead of traditional chair back, this chair was equipped with a big thread-screen on the back. The thread wall can block out the sight of the others, so as to give freedom to the person who sits behind. The threaded chair back also allows the person to look through or open it, so as to communicate with others. Moreover, it adds many playful moments in the space.

MATERIAL

Cherry wood and thread were the primary material.

CREATIVE

Peeking chair creates a new user experience. It offers privacy to the user and leaves room for communicative moments.

MAKING

The chair back was designed as a big frame. Loads of threads were glued on the upper frame to form a wall.

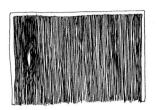

Wool Stool

DESIGN /
Hanna Bramford

CLIENT /
Lund School of Architecture

PHOTOGRAPHY /
Hanna Bramford

Wool Stool was a school project that Hanna Bramford created in the course Design Process and Prototype at Lund School of Architecture. She drew inspiration from the term "the Black Sheep"—a metaphor referring to someone who stands out from the crowd. The basic idea and concept, as Hanna said, was to explore what she could get from a black sheep.

CREATIVE

By combining traditional craft skills with the otherwise modern appearance, the designer wanted to create a piece of furniture that, like the black sheep, stands out from the crowd.

MATERIAL

The designer used wool from a black sheep for the seat of the stool. The framework is constructed of steel and wood. The legs are made of birch plywood.

MAKING

The designer started the project by carding the wool from a Gotland sheep in order to explore its characteristics and possibilities. With the same amount of wool, she felted one hundred solid wool balls that were used as the seat of the stool. As for the stool legs, she glued pieces of birch plywood together which were then processed through a certain kind of lathe machine.

Iconic Rockers

AGENCY /
Maison Deux

DESIGN /
Pia Weinberg

Iconic Rockers are the new generation of rocking horses designed and manufactured by Maison Deux. The series consists of the Iconic Cloud and the Iconic Water Melon, and the Bowler Hat Rocker, on which kids can take the joy ride. All the Iconic Rockers are crafted in the Netherlands and made from high quality, natural materials. The contrast of solid French oak and fabric made from 100% wool by Kvadrat amplifies the Iconics's quality. Rocking the Iconics emphasizes a child's coordination and balance skills. It is also the foundation for imaginative play—"Who said that a rocking horse has to be an actual horse?"

MATERIAL

Crafted from solid French oak and upholstered with 100% wool by Kvadrat. The Divina Melange 2 by Finn Sködt gives the Iconic Rockers a soft and rich look.

CREATIVE

Maison Deux wants to create designs that are both for kids and their parents, to create a modern home and living environment where both generations can live in harmony.

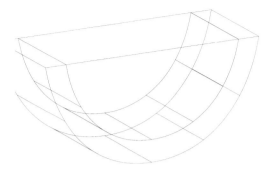

Maison Deux combines old-world craftsmanship with modern-day technology, to create a product that lasts for generations. For the wooden elements of the Iconic Rockers, a computer controlled CNC is used in combination with the human soft touch finish.

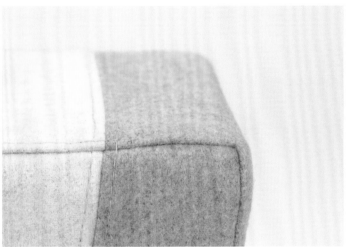

Nascondino

DESIGN /
Pierre-Emmanuel Vandeputte

"Nascondino" means "hide-and-seek" in Italian. It is a collection of alcoves providing a moment of intimacy. Reminiscent of the youthful days of hide-and-seek, Nascondino creates a new space in which users can lose themselves in reverie, alone or accompanied. When they leave their feet poking out, it is usually because they want to be found.

MAKING

The oak woods are put together with an hanger on the top. The felt is cut into circle with a hole which can be easily hanged on or removed from the frame.

MATERIAL

The frame is made of oak wood. The shade is made of natural felt.

CREATIVE

Nascondino is not only in memory of childhood, but also a portrait of modern lifestyle—people live and work together, but they also need private space.

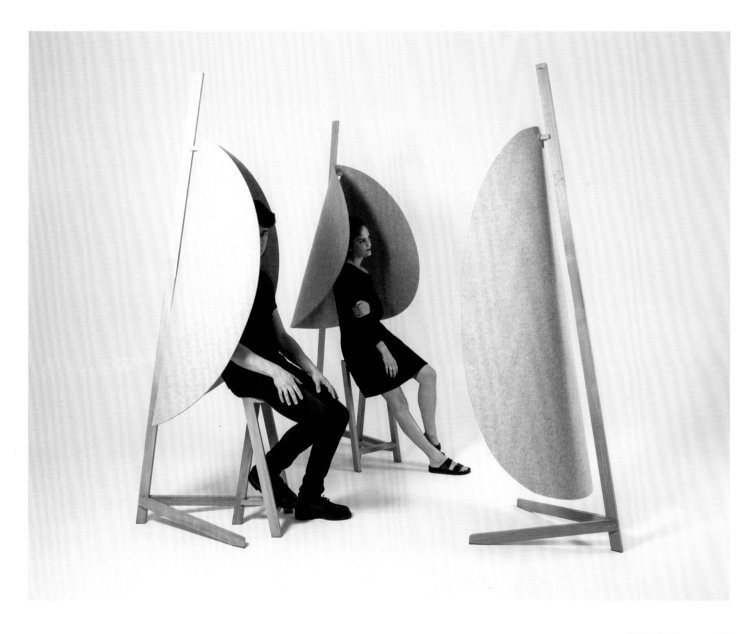

Wobble-Up

DESIGN /
Sam Linders

PHOTOGRAPHY /
Sam Linders, Sjors Kanters

"Wobble-Up" is Sam Linders's graduation project at the Design Academy Eindhoven. This project shows flexibility and playfulness in a contemporary form for an adaptable living environment. These carpets can be transformed into three-dimensional shapes to create wobbling sitting spots. The ancient craft of traditional embroidery is fused with the modern technique of mechanically punched plastic. By using blocks of color and highlighting the plastic grid, the carpets are becoming fresh and playful. The carpet can be endlessly multiplied as mosaic tiles to make it possible for the consumer to play with pattern and color. One simple incision turns the carpet into a wobbling seat. The carpets can be used in rooms with multiple functions.

CREATIVE

When at home, the designer is always sitting in front of the couch rather than on the couch when watching TV, thus he came up with the idea of the Wobble-Up. It is a product that can be used as a seat and a carpet. He really loves to sit on the carpet. Next to this, the living spaces are becoming smaller. Thus he intended to make a multi functional furniture piece that can be flat as a carpet and folded as a chair on the floor.

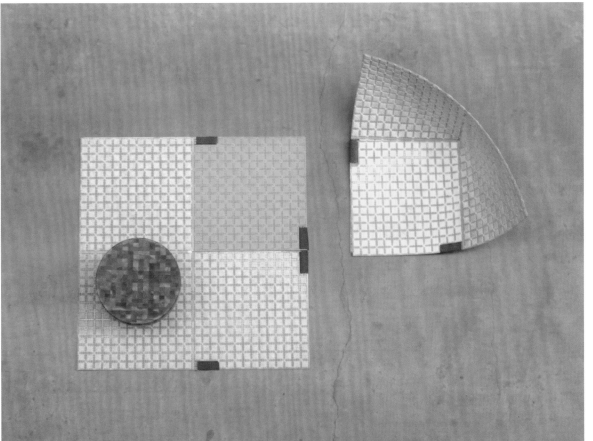

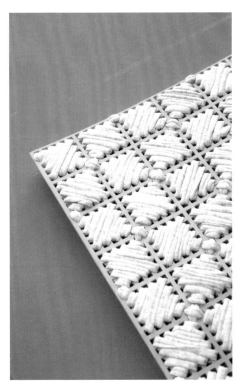

MATERIAL

These floor tiles are made of a mechanically punched plastic that is embroidered with jersey yarn for a tactile feeling. The tile can be folded into a wobbling shape and it is connected by the Velcro. The Velcro also connects the tiles together when they are flatted as a carpet.

MAKING

It is totally not about molding but about folding. A molded product out of one shape means normally that the shape is a stable form. Sam's product is about flexibility in a shape. The shape is flexible that goes from a two-dimensional tile to a three-dimensional form.

De-dimension Project

DESIGN /
Jongha Choi

PHOTOGRAPHY /
Jongha Choi

Jongha Choi has created a collection of benches and stools called "De-dimension" that can be transformed from a flat, two-dimensional view, to a three-dimension functional object. Though the image still shows its visual effect on a flat plane, but this time it is not just an expression of representation, but rather making an experience real. In modern society, people experience the image in relation to advertising, photography, film, and the Internet. Why not question an image's confinement to a flat surface? Why not try to get more stereoscopic and attempt on direct experience with the image? With these questions in mind, Jongha embarked on this project and tried to realize such ideas from his own point of view.

MATERIAL

Aluminum plates, laser cutting, powder coating, rivets, and hinges were the main materials and tools used to make De-dimension.

MAKING

Aluminum plates were put together by rivets. The seats and legs were connected by using hinges, which enabled the stools to be folded.

CREATIVE

Two-dimensional image is often shown on a flat screen, usually virtual. This project allows people to experience a two-dimensional image as a three-dimensional object in reality.

N-S STOOL

DESIGN /
Yuhao Shen

This design is based on an experiment on material by bending plywood and placing magnets underneath each veneer. N-S Stool is composed of three pieces of plywood. The three sheets of plywood are exactly the same size. The stool uses magnets instead of mechanical fasteners, which allows easy attachment and removal. Therefore, it is easy to produce and deliver.

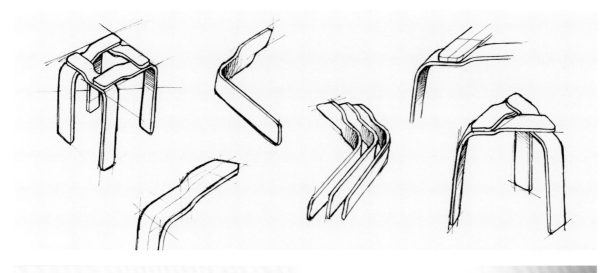

MATERIAL

Birch veneers and magnets.

MAKING

It is all about bending the plywood into the appropriate shape.

CREATIVE

A plywood stool jointed by magnet can be assembled and disassembled easily. It is easy to store, carry, and save space.

Louis Vuitton Blossom Stool

DESIGN /
Tokujin Yoshioka

A symbolic stool inspired by the Louis Vuitton monogram of petals—this stool is designed with natural structure which represents the motion of blooming petals transformed from a bud. The craftsmanship with wood and leather craftwork technique has been cultivated in the long history of the brand. This art object conveys a strong iconic message and travels beyond times, projecting the history and the future of Louis Vuitton.

MATERIAL

Wood and leather are the main material.

MAKING

The stool is assembled by hand.

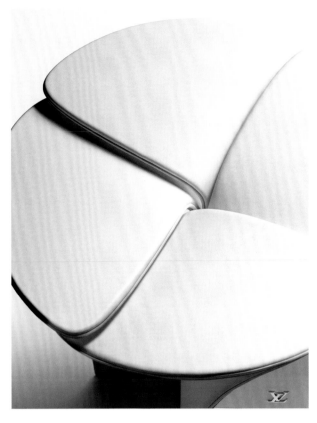

Tokujin Yoshioka always tries to invent something beyond forms. He wanted to create something iconic which strongly symbolizes the philosophy of Louis Vuitton, thus he created an object that is universal and timeless.

Dokkaebi Stool

AGENCY /
JiyounKim Studio
DESIGN /
Jiyoun Kim

"Dokkaerbi" is an imaginary monster in Korean folk stories, which is not merely a monster, but a joyful spirit that rewards the good and punishes the evil. Dokkaebi Stool were cylindrical stainless steel delicately mirror polished. Eight different gradient colors were painted on the upper part of each cylinder, representing the colors of pine tree forest in different seasons. Kim created the perceptual illusions, making the colored superior sides seem to be floating in the middle of the air. Just like Dokkaebi can easily alter his appearance, 24 Dokkaebi Stools can also transform the colors according to that of the grass, tree, and sky.

CREATIVE

With its super mirror polishing and cylinder shape, Dokkaebi Stool naturally immerses in the surroundings and convolutes depending on its distances between the viewers, reflected objects. The designer called such characteristics as Dokkaebi's prank.

MATERIAL

The stool was made of stainless steel, 4mm in thickness, each of which could be lifted by a person. It was necessary to use paints that would stay resilient to the harsh environments to which these stools were exposed. Clear coating was employed to emphasize the clear distinction of the super mirror polished part.

MAKING

Kim selected a small site where 24 pine trees were planted. Each stool was installed beside a pine tree. The size of the stools was kept uniform: 355 × 355 × 470mm, since the designer wanted to emphasize the gradient colors as the only variation between the stools, while at the same time to ensure that the stools could serve as art installations as well as usable furniture.

Sand Furniture

AGENCY /
alien and monkey

Sand Furniture is part of alien and monkey's "Sand Made Project," a series of designs that continue to explore this new sustainable material, including Sand Packaging and Sand Light. The design concept stems from the Freudian idea that the loss of objects awakens memories and emotions within their owner. A product's physical evolution caused by time and its owner's mishaps will create deeper emotional bonds between them. Ephemeral in essence, the Sand furniture can last for a long period of time, and slowly crumble back to dust at the end of their lives, leaving behind just grains of sand and other minerals that are harmless to the environment.

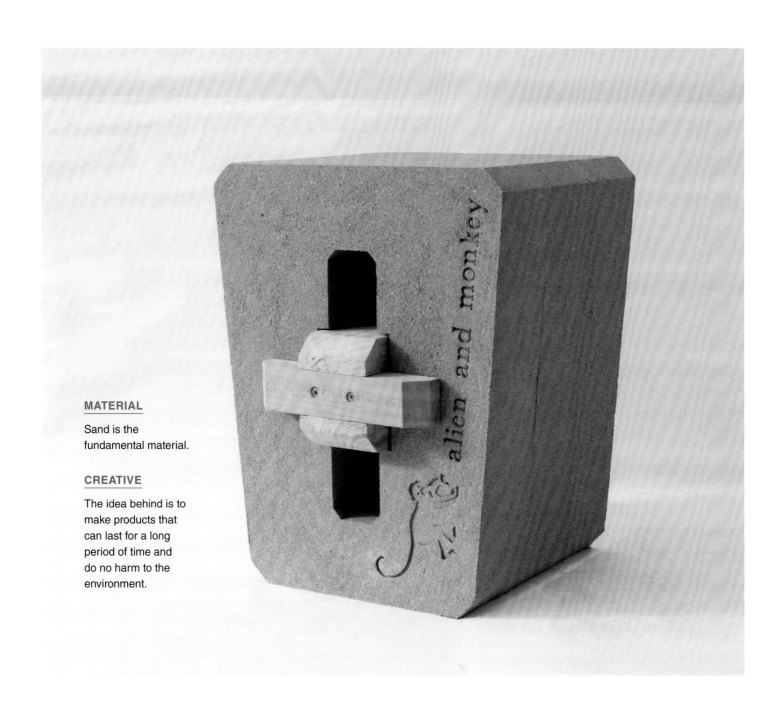

MATERIAL

Sand is the fundamental material.

CREATIVE

The idea behind is to make products that can last for a long period of time and do no harm to the environment.

MAKING

Employing a traditional process and a touch of alchemy, particles of sand are shaped and formed into objects. By varying the specifics of the process, like pressure, temperature, percentage of added minerals, different properties of longevity and strength can be developed so as to modify the material to suit different applications.

Straw Stool

DESIGN /
Juan Cappa

Straw is a forgotten material, even though it has been widely used in past times as building material in thatched roofs and wall insulation, or as filling material in furniture and upholstery such as mattress. So why not use this easily accessible material in a new and more direct way in which material is actually in contact with our body.

The stools are made by holding straws tightly packed in a metal structure. The compact packing of a big bundle of straws transforms the weak straw into a strong and comfortable surface. The straws are loose inside the structure, making the surface resilient and allowing the straws to move when the user sits on it.

MATERIAL

The structure is made of metal. The seat is made of birch plywood and loads of straws.

MAKING

The straws are tightly packed in a metal frame.

CREATIVE

The well-known insulating properties of straw create a warm and breathable surface when in use.

TABURET

DESIGN /
Anastasiya Koshcheeva

Taburet is a stool with a three-dimensional seat made of birch bark stripes, sewed and fixed together on a steel frame. The stool is 32cm wide, 32cm deep, and 45cm high. The stable, light, and elastic meshwork looks different from every angle and builds an optical illusion, cushioning the stool in a decorative and comfortable way.

MATERIAL

The frame is made of steel. The seat is made of birch bark.

MAKING

The birch bark stripes are sewed together by hand.

CREATIVE

The design has turned an age-old Siberian craft into contemporary design.

PaperBricks Series

AGENCY /
Studio Woojai

DESIGN /
Woojai Lee

Paperbricks is comprised of Pallet series and Sculpt series. Paperbricks are made from recycled newspaper pulp that has been mixed with glue and pressed into a mould. The paper lends the bricks a textured and marbled exterior, which at the same time, carries the warmth and soft tactility of the paper. Pallet series is a set of well-assembled benches and tables. The tabletops are made of horizontally placed blocks, while the bricks are placed vertically on their ends as the legs to support the tops. To explore the possibilities of the bricks, Lee has created the Sculpt series. Paper can be both soft and hard, rough and smooth, systematic and irregular. The soft surface and rigid shape are in contrast to the rough and natural forms.

CREATIVE

It explores the different qualities of the material "paper." The form of the bricks was chosen to minimize the material usage, minimize the deformation, and maximize strength.

MATERIAL

Newspaper and wood glue are the fundamental material.

MAKING

The newspaper pulp has been mixed with glue and pressed into a mould to make a brick. Each brick can be cut, drilled, and glued in the similar way as wood. There are holes on the undersurface of each block, allowing the blocks to be jointed together.

L+P

DESIGN /
Elena Rogna

The project is based on the desire to combine wood and plastic in the same creative process. The letter "L" refers to the Italian word "legno," which means "wood;" the letter "P" is from the word "plastic." Thus the project is given the name "L+P." The aim is to realize a structure that is very light regardless of the mixture of two different materials. The two material are usually shaped separately. "L+P" is dedicated to the trend market: restaurants, hotels, and concept stores.

CREATIVE

It fits modern aesthetics with the clean shape.

MATERIAL

The plastic soul of L+P is made of polyethylene. The beech wood is selected for its color, clean and neutral surface scarcely with deep veins. Such wood is almost a perfect fit for plastic shells of any color.

MAKING

The two materials are perfectly jointed together. The chair seat has applied a new technology: the simultaneous injection of wood and polyethylene by pressing the shell onto the ends of beech wood. The shape of the shell has an ergonomic convexity and side pockets for pilling up. The legs are glued later.

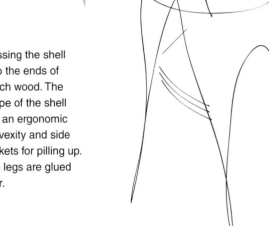

Sibirjak

DESIGN /
Anastasiya Koshcheeva

Sibirjak is a contemporary lounge chair made of birch bark. The fascinating natural material is not only flexible, soft, water-repellent and antibacterial, but also breathable, durable and strong. Despite these unique characteristics, it gets gradually forgotten. In response, Sibirjak deals with the questions of how to reinterpret an age-old tradition and how to make the conventional handcraft up-to-date.

The chair and ottoman combination emphasize the material's aesthetics, combining traditional skills with modern processing. The horizontal alignment of the bark underlines the leather-like properties of the material, offering a wide comfortable seat. The textile details and the reduced geometric frame form a strong contrast to the natural birch bark.

MATERIAL

The frame is made of steel. The seat is made of birch bark. The dimensions of the chair is 70cm wide, 45cm deep, and 36/70cm high; the dimensions of the ottoman is 70cm wide, 40cm deep, and 36cm high.

MAKING

The biggest available pieces of birch bark are carefully selected and prepared by hand.

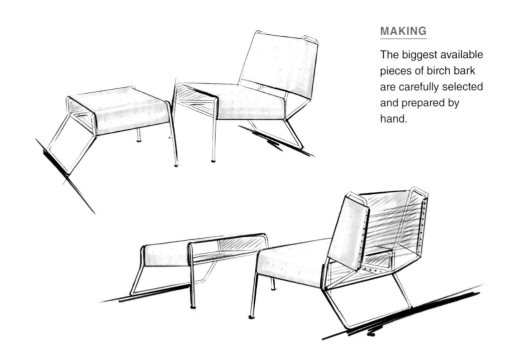

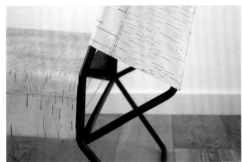

CREATIVE

The design has turned an age-old Siberian craft into contemporary design.

Block Bench Armed

AGENCY /
Sitskie

DESIGN /
Adam Friedman

The objective of the cushioned Block system is to give the user a soft comfortable experience while keeping all the benefits of a solid surface—durability, cleanliness and the beauty of the solid material, in this case wood. The designer has learned that people have a love/hate relationship with upholstered furniture. Along with the softness of an upholstered piece comes the natural concerns about damage, staining, dust, life of the fabric, and longevity of the style. The inability to truly get any upholstered product clean without removing covers and going to great lengths is an inescapable reality and a bitter pill to swallow. Through years of trial and error, the Block system is now a unique solution backed by a U.S. patent.

CREATIVE

The experience of the Block Bench compressing and forming to the body is unlike any other chair. The designers have scrutinized over comfort—it is always the first concern, and as a result these chairs will hold the users comfortably for hours.

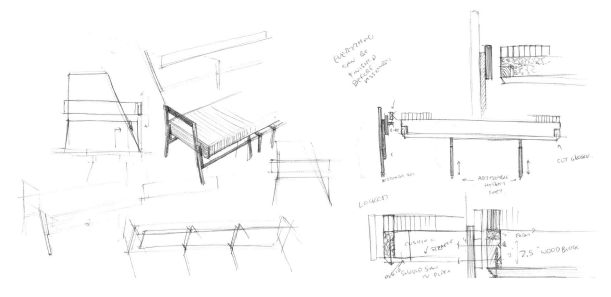

MATERIAL

Each chair is made from solid domestic walnut hardwood. Wood is responsibly harvested—FSC Certified. The upholstery is made of foam and fabric.

MAKING

Everything is hand made in Detroit by local independent artisans and businesses.

Needle Chair &
Woven Pendant

AGENCY /
Veega Design

London-based designer Veega Tankun possesses a strong sense of aesthetic and understanding of materials as evidenced in her signature chairs and pendants from overstuffed knit tubes with comfy looking. Tankun is passionate about rejuvenating old techniques in her design practice, bringing modern materials and color palettes to traditional production methods. The size of the chair is 76cm in width, 85cm in height, and 110cm in depth; the pendant is 16.5cm in width, 19-25cm in height.

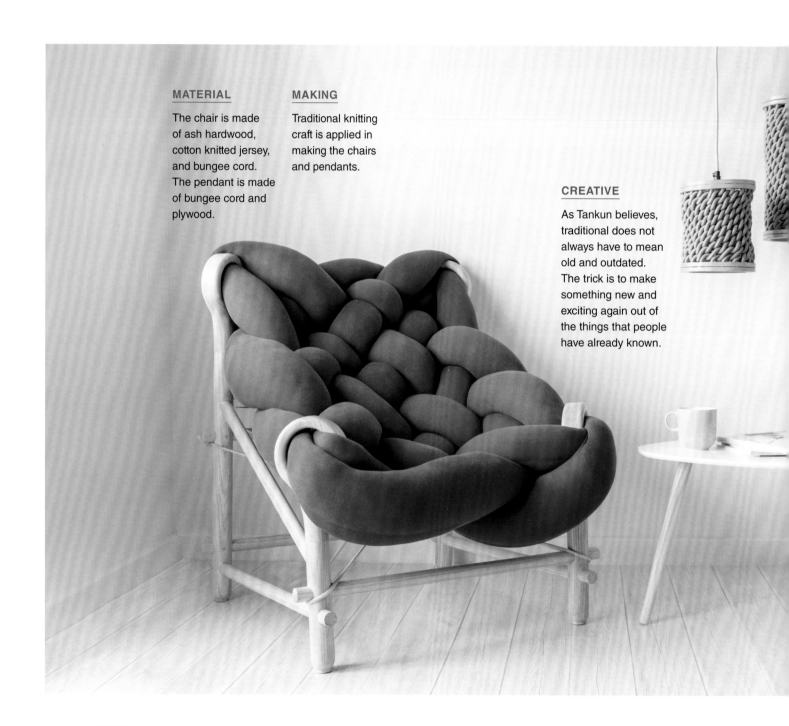

MATERIAL

The chair is made of ash hardwood, cotton knitted jersey, and bungee cord. The pendant is made of bungee cord and plywood.

MAKING

Traditional knitting craft is applied in making the chairs and pendants.

CREATIVE

As Tankun believes, traditional does not always have to mean old and outdated. The trick is to make something new and exciting again out of the things that people have already known.

Dolcefarniente—Calla

AGENCY /
Fritsch-Durisotti

Made with natural wicker, Dolcefarniente—Calla gives a new approach to traditional wicker furniture with a fun and uncluttered style by mixing metal and natural fiber. This creation is the beginning of a new range that includes a double armchair, table, coffee table.

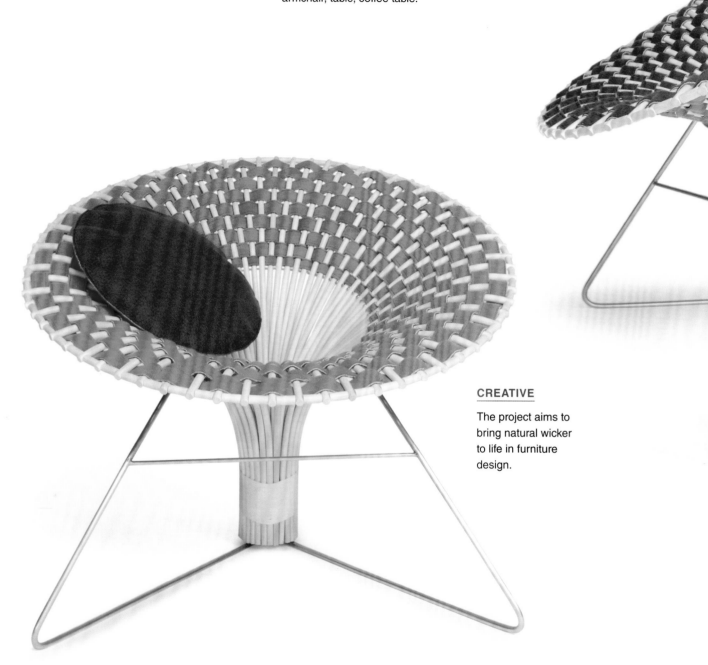

CREATIVE

The project aims to bring natural wicker to life in furniture design.

MATERIAL

Natural wicker and metal are the main material.

MAKING

Wickers are woven with colorful straps by applying traditional knitting technique.

Du Côté de Chez Vous—Drôles d'Oiseaux

AGENCY /
Fritsch-Durisotti

"Drôles d'Oiseaux" means "funny birds" in French. The series consists of a set of furniture and lighting devices including armchair, ottoman, floor lamp, and clothes rack. The projects have been presented at the design community event "Du Côté de Chez Vous." In this series, Fritsch-Durisotti has combined the traditional knitting craft with the high-end 3D printing technique. Each product is given a name corresponding a type of bird. The armchair featured below is called "nightingale," and the ottoman "chicken."

MATERIAL

Wood and synthetic fiber are the main material.

CREATIVE

The projects explores the possibilities of different materials and crafts.

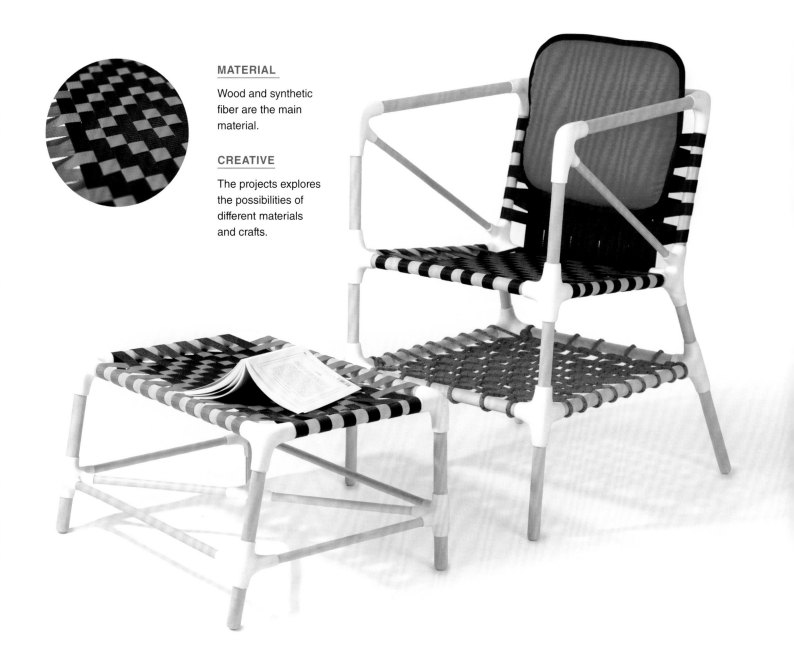

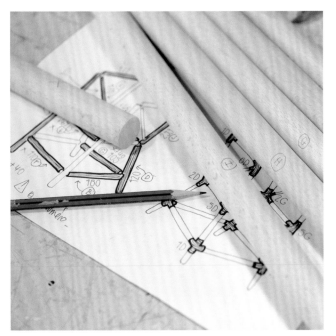

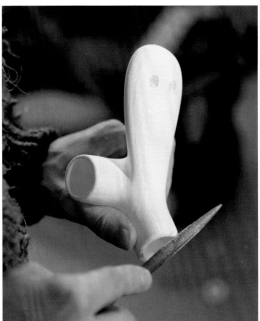

The seat of the armchair and ottoman is made by knitting the synthetic fiber. The frame made of wood are assembled using connecting joints manufactured by 3D printing technique.

Objet-O

AGENCY /
SY DESIGN

DESIGN /
Seung-Yong Song

PHOTOGRAPHY /
Jun-Ho Yum

Objet-O is a chair with huge lampshade above. It looks like a bird's nest from afar. The designer drew inspiration from his childhood memory. He used to make a den somewhere in his house when he was a kid—the den could be under the table, in the wardrobe, or in the attic. He created his own base and felt relieved as if he was avoiding enemies. Objet-O resembles a secret space for the users, where they can feel safe and cozy.

MATERIAL

The size of the chair is 1800 × 1800 × 2200mm. The chair is made of white birch. The lamp shape is made of Korean traditional papers and painted with UV gloss paint.

MAKING

Steel wire and wood are shaped as the frame of the lamp shade. The paper is cut into pieces, which are glued piece by piece to make the shade.

CREATIVE

The lamp shade can be scaled up or down. When it is scaled down, the user can stay quietly in the midst of the nest-like shade, enjoying his or her own time by reading, listening to music, or simply meditating.

Salangbang

AGENCY /
SY DESIGN

DESIGN /
Seung-Yong Song

PHOTOGRAPHY /
Jun-Ho Yum

There was no fence or gate where the designer used to live. Opening the doors, the cottage was surrounded by the yard, streams, and nature. The designer drew inspiration from the cottage in past and created Sarangbang. In Korea, Sarangbang is a type of room located in a Korean traditional house, which usually serves as man's room, used for studying, writing poetry, and leisure activities. The same type of two objects may face each other, stand side by side, or stand alone. By opening and closing the door, space can be either connected or divided.

MATERIAL

The dimension of the furniture is1400 × 850 × 1740mm. White birch, Korean paper, and mixed materials are used.

MAKING

All making are
processed by hand.

CREATIVE

Within an extensive
space, it is possible
to create a cozy
space of one's own.

Nap Bar: Dunes

AGENCY /
smarin

DESIGN /
Stephanie Marin

Nap Bar draws inspiration from a recovery moment, a quasi-universal tradition known in many cultures: nap, a simple and intuitive exercise. In the Nap Bar, speech is silver; silence is gold. Voices are softened; phones are closed. Dunes is a series of lounge chairs in the Nap Bar. The shapes are drawn to induce a situation of letting go, giving the user therapeutic experience with psychological and physical benefits. The users can read, sit, or dream on their Dunes. There are three shapes available for Dunes: Erg, Barkhane, and Nebka, allowing the users to choose from a variable compositions.

MAKING

The chairs are all shaped specially to guarantee a high level of comfort.

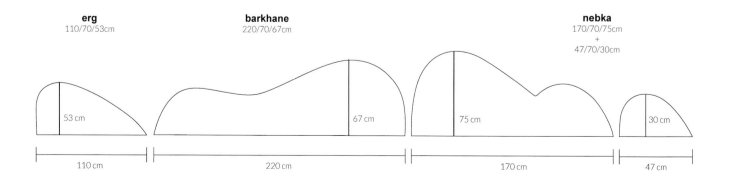

erg
110/70/53cm

53 cm

110 cm

barkhane
220/70/67cm

67 cm

220 cm

nebka
170/70/75cm
+
47/70/30cm

75 cm

30 cm

170 cm

47 cm

MATERIAL

The chairs are
made out of foam
of different density
for perfect support.
Kvadrat's fabric-100%
polyester is used.

CREATIVE

The Dunes in the
Nap Bar offers a
moment of quietness
and coziness for
users.

Tenderwood

DESIGN /
Yenhao Chu

PHOTOGRAPHY /
Anastasia Mityukova

Wooden chairs are usually elegant and neat; however, it is difficult to sit on them for too long. Therefore, a cushion is always placed on the chair. But what if a wooden chair becomes soft and still keeps the aesthetic of wood? After running several experiments, the designer has found a way to achieve this. With the combination of three-dimensional pressed flexible wood veneer and soft foam, the sitting surface provides subtle softness.

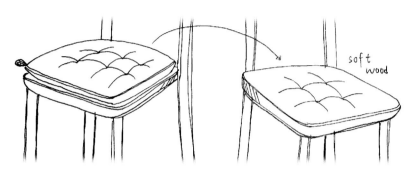

MAKING

The concept of "flexible and durable" sitting surface has been achieved by applying natural wood veneer with flexible coating and gluing.

MATERIAL

The chair is made of wood and soft foam.

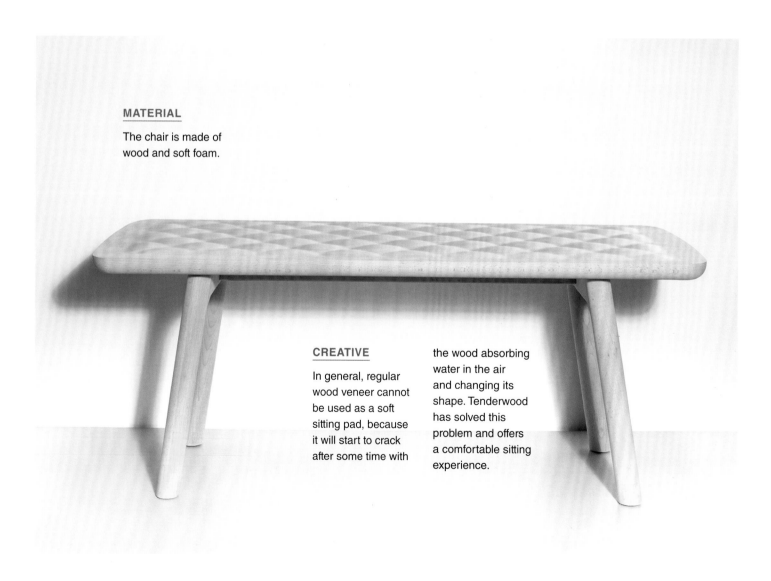

CREATIVE

In general, regular wood veneer cannot be used as a soft sitting pad, because it will start to crack after some time with the wood absorbing water in the air and changing its shape. Tenderwood has solved this problem and offers a comfortable sitting experience.

Moon Lattice Hanger

DESIGN /
Yenhao Chu

This product can serves as a causal hanger to drape over scarves, neckties, accessories, and prepared clothes. Its form is an implication of moon lattice which is a type of window widely used in traditional Chinese architectures. Instead of implanting a lot of design into a product, the designers have chosen the simple and beautiful "cross section" of bamboo to act as holders.

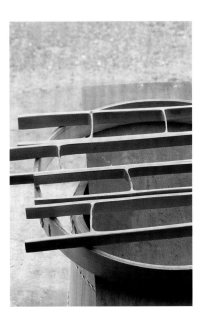

MATERIAL

Bamboo is the main material.

MAKING

Manufacturing technique of bamboo has been used.

CREATIVE

The shape and structure renders the hanger a picturesque scenery with or without garments on it.

jià

DESIGN /
Ken Chen

ART DIRECTION /
Tom Weis

PHOTOGRAPHY /
Yoon Shik Kim

Ken Chen drew inspiration from a basin rack made during Ming Dynasty and created "jià," a vanity dresser that offered functionality to fit into modern scenarios. The traditional basin rack used to be a pear wood rack where people could place a wash basin. People would use it to wash their face before starting the day. It had a very well-balance proportion and appealing color. In order to add more functions while keeping the same proportion, Ken added components such as a drawer, a small shelf, and a rack, which improved the practicality of the design. Unlike a conventional mirror, the polished copper created a unique filter that beautified the mirror image. With "jià," Ken seeks to transcend the current Western-influenced space and reintroduces Asian style to a common home area.

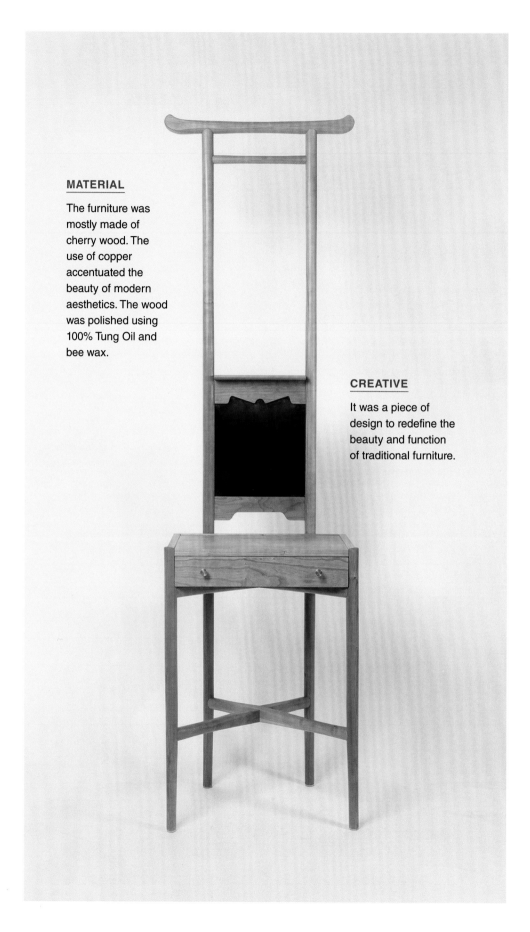

MATERIAL

The furniture was mostly made of cherry wood. The use of copper accentuated the beauty of modern aesthetics. The wood was polished using 100% Tung Oil and bee wax.

CREATIVE

It was a piece of design to redefine the beauty and function of traditional furniture.

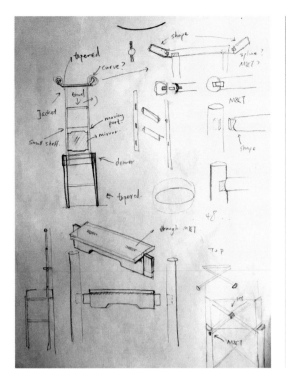

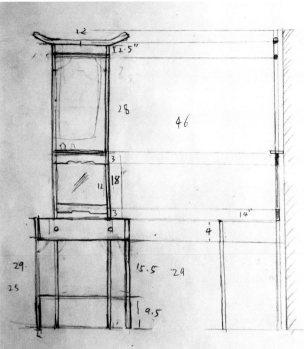

Most work were involved in woodworking. The piece was completely constructed using traditional joinery. Square pieces were carefully carved and shaped down into subtle curves.

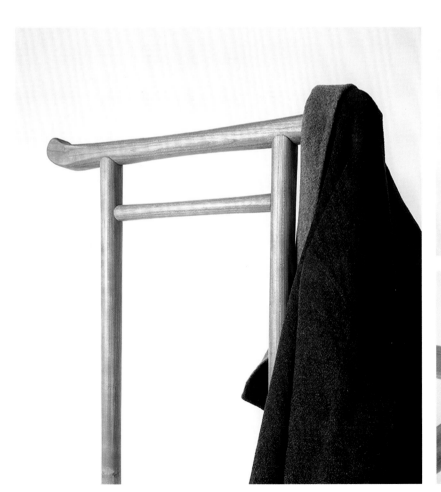

"IXA" Chest of Drawers Design

DESIGN /
Vaidas Byla

Vaidas Byla has designed "IXA" during his study at Vilnius Art Academy Kaunas Faculty. "IXA" is a minimal chest of drawers. It is designed from two geometric forms—triangle and rectangle, so as to make the idea of geometrical intersection. The shape makes the "IXA" notable and different.

MATERAIL

The furniture is made from plywood.

MAKING

All making has been done by hand.

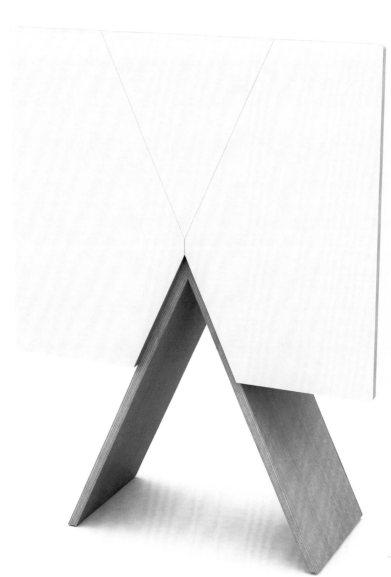

CREATIVE

There is no handles on the drawers, which makes "IXA" more minimal and aesthetic.

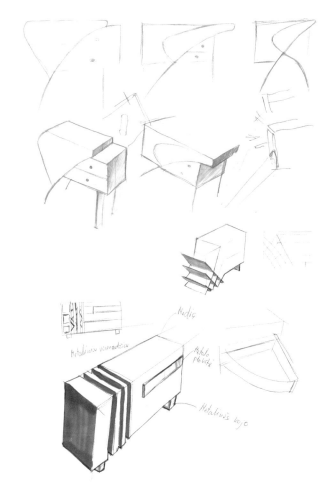

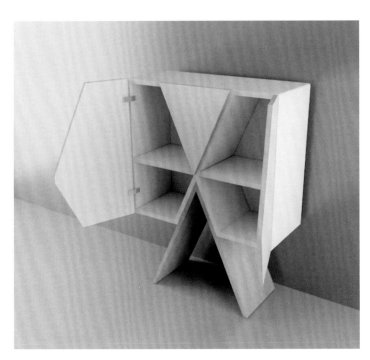

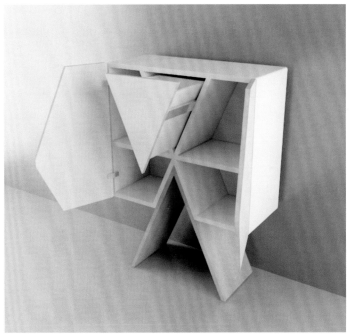

1/2 Coffee Table

AGENCY /
ziinlife

PHOTOGRAPHY /
ziinlife

"1/2" is a small coffee table, while its functionality can be doubled. The coffee table is separated by an artful slash, which provides visual balance as well as extendable functionality. This artful separation enables articles of various heights to be easily accommodated in the lower half. The users can easily change its length, or freely turn the 1/2 piece to adjust to the surrounding sittings.

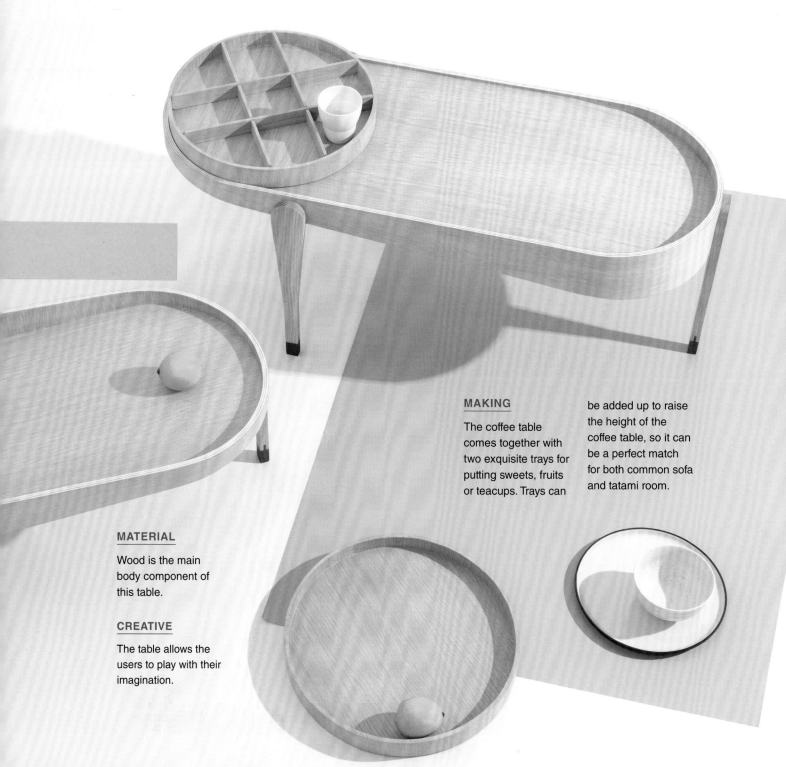

MAKING

The coffee table comes together with two exquisite trays for putting sweets, fruits or teacups. Trays can be added up to raise the height of the coffee table, so it can be a perfect match for both common sofa and tatami room.

MATERIAL

Wood is the main body component of this table.

CREATIVE

The table allows the users to play with their imagination.

Dali Round Table

AGENCY /
ziinlife

PHOTOGRAPHY /
ziinlife

Dali is an interesting round table that interacts with the wall in an artful way. Dali takes traditional bamboo slips as its inspiration, realized by ingeniously utilizing common materials. Its inclined end enables a round table to seamlessly melt into the wall, which is a perfect size for compact living. Dali can be easily switched back to its original size to welcome more guests.

MAKING

The table is put together by traditional joinery.

MATERIAL

Wood is the main body component of this table.

CREATIVE

The folding side can incline to the wall, so that the table can be adjusted to fit different room size.

Sfrido

DESIGN /
Carlo Contin

PHOTOGRAPHY /
Andrea Basile

Sfrido is a series of tables, which Carlo Contin realized using semi-finished scraps of wood waste. Usually these scraps of wood are used in the furniture industry to make decorative elements, moldings, covers, handrails, skirting boards, etc.

The designer has collected the wood to come up with some tables with extraordinary textures and patterns. The final project has been exhibited at the exhibition "Here We Go Again" curated by Stefano Maffei at the gallery Subalterno1 in Milan.

MATERIAL

The main material is wood. Glue and band saw are used during the manufacture.

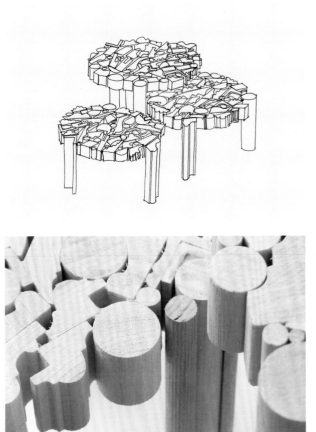

MAKING

Scrap woods are glued together and cut vertically using band saw.

CREATIVE

With pieces of wood glued together, each table is adorned with random yet natural patterns.

Tier

DESIGN /
Virosh Rangalla

Incorporating a hanging light, Tier pushes the boundaries of what a side table could be. The concept began as a study of different configurations of a side table concept, considering height, stance, and additional functionality. This idea of building upwards while maintaining a small footprint provided the structure with a hanging light source which could provide ambient lighting when needed. Due to the number of components, emphasis was placed on unique and complimentary CMF (color, material, finishing), as well as simple assembly.

MATERIAL

The platforms are make of painted beech wood for its light weight and machinability. The legs could be a number of hardwoods including maple, oak, or teak. The light cord would be wrapped in nylon and the fixture itself would be an ABS plastic housing with an Edison style bulb.

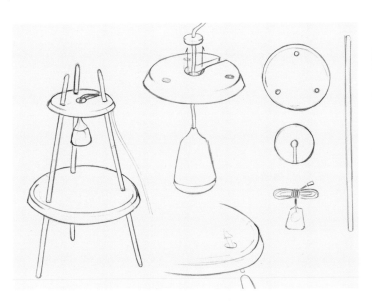

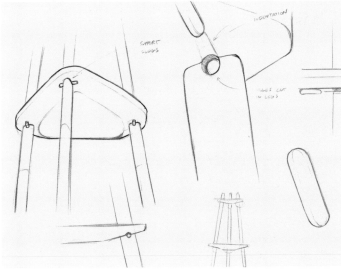

MAKING

The tier platforms would be manufactured using a CNC then finished by hand. The legs would be machined from pre-cut planks.

CREATIVE

This new concept for side table enables easy assembly and disassembly by utilizing pegs as fasteners to hold the platforms in place.

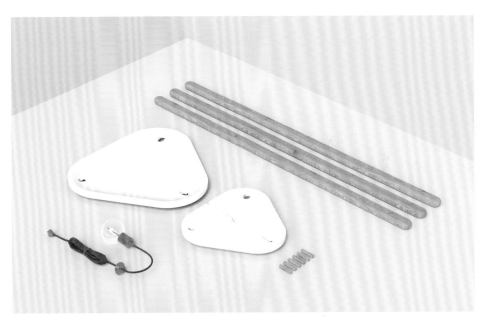

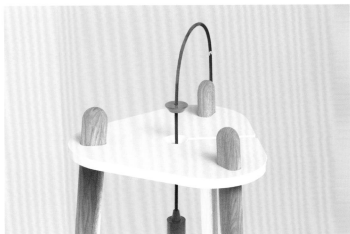

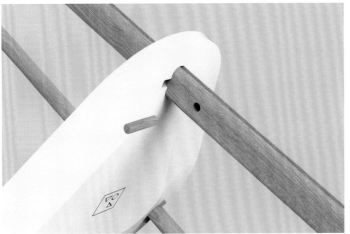

Lumber

AGENCY /
Design Studio PESI.

PHOTOGRAPHY /
Park Yoon

PESI designed a self-making side table collection, named "Lumber," using only simple processed cardboards and PVC rivets. The project was approached for a purpose of new usability and expandability of a cardboard.

A total of eleven pieces of rectangular lumbers assembled in various ways can form one of the six types of tables. Colors and patterns can be freely printed on cardboards, therefore, it is easy to give the table a custom look.

MATERIAL

A cardboard cut by die-cutting press and some PVC rivets are the principal materials of Lumber.

CREATIVE

The side table collection is a new way to reinterpret the cardboard. It allows everyone to put together a table at home easily.

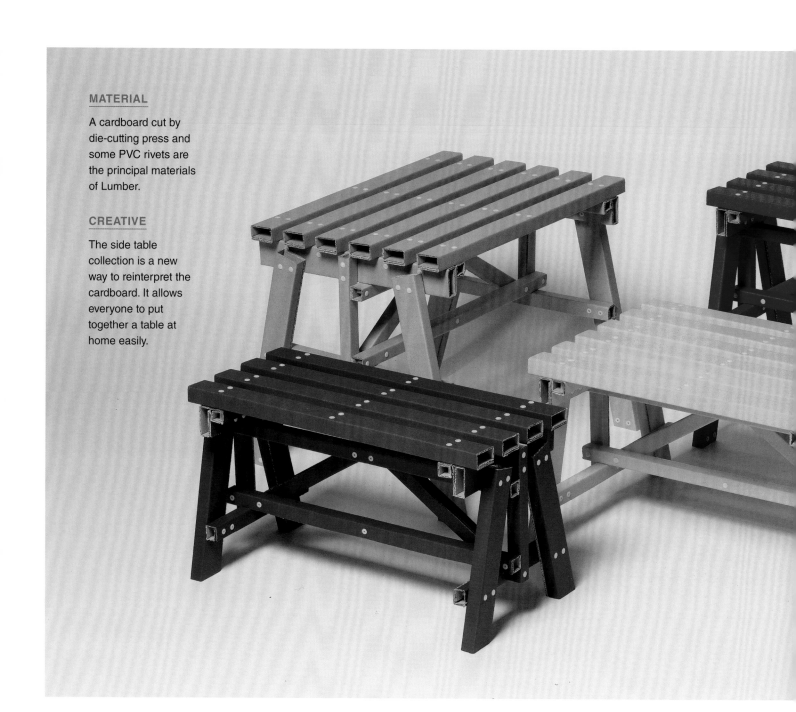

MAKING

To assemble Lumber, the cardboard is cut using die-cutting press. Each piece of processed cardboard is folded and rolled into the shape of a piece of lumber, a rectangular lumber, and held together with the PVC rivets.

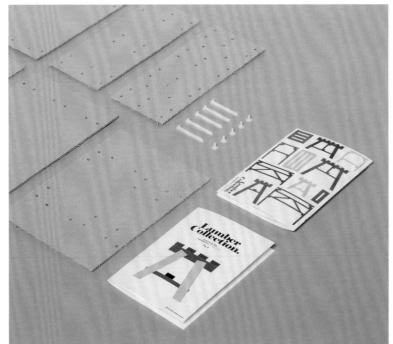

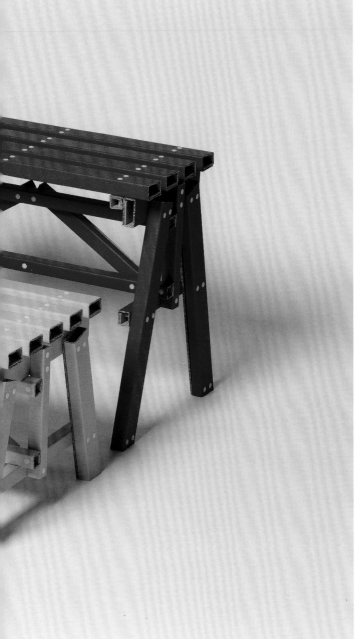

Ostrich Side Table

AGENCY /
Mario Tsai Studio

DESIGN /
Mario Tsai

CLIENT /
Valsecchi 1918

Ostrich Side Table can double as lamp. The table is designed to look like an ostrich, with its body being the table and head the lamp. The lamp can be adjusted to desirable angles and heights freely. The wood neck are put on the side of iron body, so there can be some interaction between the users with Ostrich. Ostrich Side Table could be put next to sofa or reading chair.

CREATIVE

Interesting choices in shape, style, and color have made the table a bright and fun object in living space.

MATERIAL

The body of Ostrich is made of iron, and the legs and neck are of American ash. Some magnets are put inside the wood neck to make it adjustable.

MAKING

The process involves mostly metal processing and wood processing.

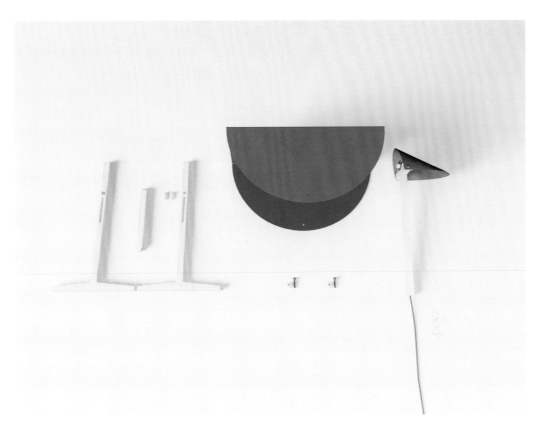

Monolitos Collection

AGENCY /
Hiperobjetos

DESIGN /
Herminio Menchaca

MANUFACTURE /
Fukui Yogyo Co., Ltd., Kurikyu Magewappa, Morimoto Kazari, Miyazaki Mokuzai Wood Industries

PHOTOGRAPHY /
Herminio Menchaca

Monolitos collections were based on the use of a type of stone from Japan called Shakudani stone, which bears some resemblance of wood. Monolitos integrated two different styles, representing Japan as a country that adapts to Western customs and preserves essential details of its own culture. The collection was comprised of coffee and side table, Torii standing lamp, and Ozen table. The wood structure of the tables and joinery were inspired by the roofs of the Shinto temples, a traditional Japanese structure to house one or more Shinto (sacred objects). "Ozen table" refers to individual tables that are used by a family, in which people can store items inside of it. "Torii standing lamps" marks the entrance of the sacred Shinto shrine.

MATERIAL

The tables were made of Shakudani stone and Japanese Cypress. Torii standing lamp and Ozen table were made of wood stone, Shakudani stone, akita cedar, brass sheet, washi (Japanese paper).

MAKING/

The process involved stone sculpting and stone turning lathe technique. Some traditional Japanese crafts and techniques were employed in woodworking, such as Kyo-sashimono, Magewappa.

CREATIVE

Hiperobjetos focused on materials and techniques with great potential to be used for daily use products, in order that craftsmanship and traditional materials can be passed down to next generations.

Avvitamenti

DESIGN /
Carlo Contin

PHOTOGRAPHY /
Andrea Basile

Avvitamenti originates from the desire
to restore traditional wood screws.
It is a collection of furniture created
for the exhibition "Avvitamenti" at
the gallery Subalterno1. The whole
collection includes lamps, tables, and
chairs. All objects are constructed of
turned wood screws.

CREATIVE

The structural system
shows a repeatable
pattern that
conceives a variety
of household items,
from tables to desk
lamps. The series of
objects thrive on the
action of screwing.

MATERIAL

The main materials are beech wood and metal. The pieces are processed in the lathe.

MAKING

All parts are connected by turning the wood screws.

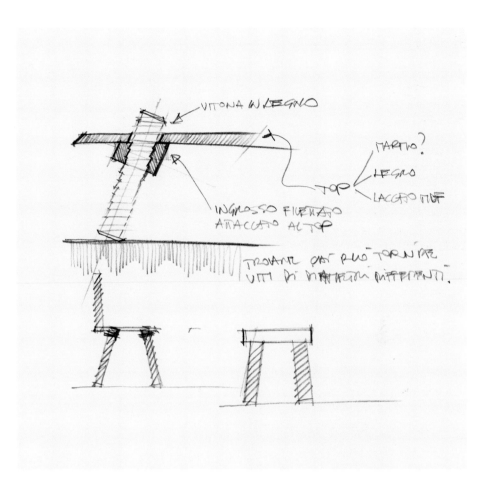

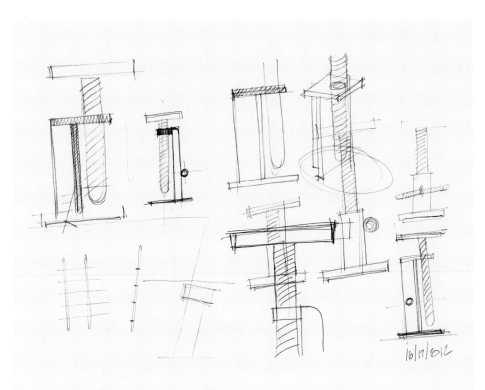

Icicle table

DESIGN /
Tianzhu Zhang

Simplicity and hidden details give the design a secret beauty waiting people to explore and experience. The legs are the frame and the top becomes a lid to cap it underneath. The feature form is inspired by icicle from nature, and created by Generative design approach.

MATERIAL

The main materials are porcelain, marble, and metal.

MAKING

The process involves steel working and ceramic molding.

CREATIVE

The product is suitable in modern minimalist interior design, making observers feel calm and peaceful.

PLEATS Shelf

DESIGN /
Shinya Oguchi

PHOTOGRAPHY /
Shinya Oguchi

PLEATS is a shelf made of cardboard. The cardboard is just 0.7mm in thickness, but thanks to the accordion folding structure, the shelf can bear heavy stuff like books and heavy objects. The unique structure makes it possible for the users to fold up the shelf, so as to minimize the volume and store it in a tiny space. It can be stretched and extended to a maximum depth of 300mm. The zigzagging shape not only serves as the structure but also a joint part. The shelves can be easy to connect with one another. There are three colors available for the shelves: gray, dark gray, and blue, which can fit any kinds of rooms. The prototypes were made by FUKUNAGA PRINT.

CREATIVE

It is a piece of design that combines modern aesthetics, functionality, and environmental protection.

MATERIAL

Cardboard is the only material used.

MAKING

It requires folding along a set of predefined creases on the cardboard.

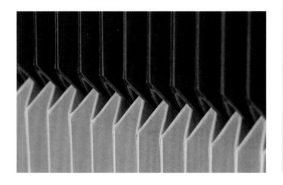

Wood Mosaic: Furniture

AGENCY /
KAIRI EGUCHI DESIGN

DESIGN /
Kairi Eguchi, Enya Hou

MANUFACTURE /
Brio Inc.

PHOTOGRAPHY /
Manabu Sato

"Beautiful Remnants—Valuing the beauty of remnants over lumber." The wood that the designers use as material is lumbered. In the manufacturing process of furniture, there are some parts left out: the remnants. Even though they are harvested from the same tree, remnants are marked as low-value from the start. The designers' intention was to create something beautiful out of these remnants—something more beautiful than being made out of lumber. Their thoughts went into the hopes of raising the value of remnants, leading to a new door for an environmental-friendly product making. This series consists of furniture and lighting, all developed under the concept of "Remnants is more beautiful than lumber."

CREATIVE

It is all about the idea of valuing the beauty of remnants over lumber. The designers believe in nature beauty. Other than that, the furniture collection is ultra lightweight, which is easy to lift and tends to have lower transportation costs.

MATERIAL

The top board is made of cedar chip and urethane. The legs are of beech wood. The frame is constructed mainly with steel. The paint used is emulsion in consideration of the environment.

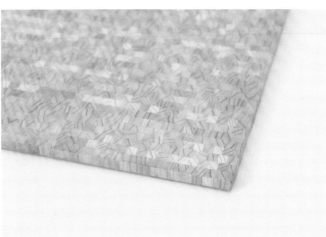

MAKING

The whole series was made out of remnants of Japanese cedar in block shapes, which then was put together in mosaic. The top board run through a process of cutting, pasting, compressing, and finishing coating. The legs were cut accordingly and finished with oil. Steel was cut using laser to form the frame of the furniture.

Cirkel
Collection

AGENCY /
Daphna Laurens

PHOTOGRAPHY /
Mike Roelofs

The "Cirkel Collection," originally edited as gallery pieces by Galerie Gosserez in Paris, consists of two wall lights, a coffee table, three mirrors, and a leaning lamp. The pieces in the collection have a shared basis: the circle. Composing, cutting, twisting the surface, adding or removing lines, and applying materials and colors resulted in the design of this collection.

MATERIAL

The main materials are aluminum and woods. There are three kinds of wood used in this collection, namely oak, walnut, and ash.

CREATIVE

The designers' interest in and admiration for bygone generations of artist, in the field of design as well as fine art, are very likely to be "visible" in the design of Cirkel collection.

MAKING

The aluminum is powder coated. The lights and coffee tables are shaped with walnut and ash veneer. Mirrors are designed in three different shape with three different woods—oak, walnut, and ash.

Pull Me to Life

DESIGN /
Juno Jeon

PHOTOGRAPHY /
Juno Jeon

Living in a space full of different kinds of objects, Juno Jeon believed that people are living together with the objects. But he questioned the extent that we interact and communicate with these objects. Instead of viewing objects as something standing still in the corner, he imagined that all objects were alive, which could make people's routines special. "Pull Me to Life" is s series of table and drawers with a textured surface which resembles "scales" on some strange creature. When the drawers is pulled, the "scales" gradually moves and changes the color from back to front. This humor-infused project aims to create a relationship between living space, objects, and human beings.

MATERIAL

Wallnut wood, beech wood, and metal wire are used in this project.

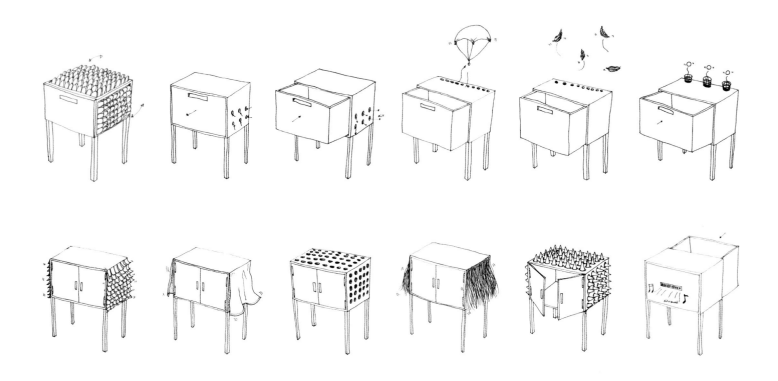

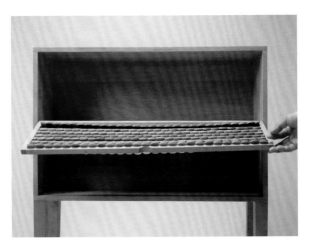

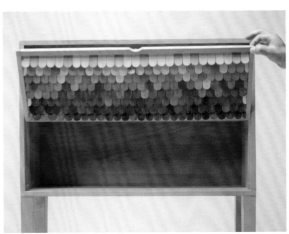

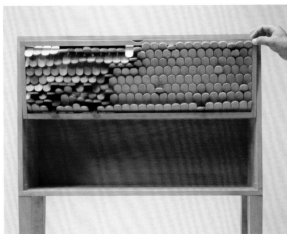

MAKING

The "scales" are made of wood and painted with desirable colors. The designer put them together by using metal wires.

CREATIVE

By making the drawers interact and communicate with their users, the designer aspired to make people's life richer.

Coiling the Unwanted

DESIGN /
Juan Cappa

Invasive species of plants, unwanted and waste materials are a challenging problem that increases and affects every continent. Coiling is a basketry technique that is used globally, and can be done with almost any material and without tools. These tables are made using very simple tools. They can be easily packed and assembled by using rope and a tourniquet to tighten the structure.

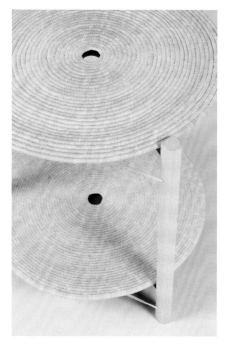

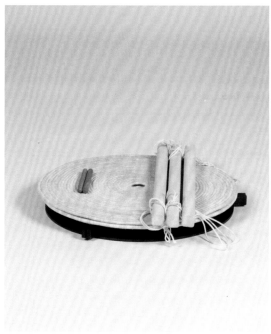

MATERIAL

Ash, birch and oak wood, water hyacinth, grass, and banana fibers are chosen. The materials mainly come from Colombia, Kenya and Sweden.

MAKING

It involves a process of basketry and woodworking.

CREATIVE

By combining the unwanted materials with a universal basketry technique, the waste problem can be addressed and generates an income for the communities affected by this problem.

Wood Caravane for Cat

DESIGN /
Jaejin Lee

PHOTOGRAPHY /
Jaejin Lee

Seeing cats have their own territory reminds the designer the images of "journey," "travel," and "deviance." Wood Caravan for cats is designed to give the users a feeling of traveling wherever they are. If the user looks at a cat sleeping inside, the user may feel as if he or she is taking a break while traveling.

CREATIVE

The product will give cats a lovely home to stay and play with.

MATERIAL

Birch plywood, leather texture fabric, and aluminum are used.

MAKING

The creating process has run through sketching, three-dimensional modeling, structure calculation, floor plan making, CNC machine cutting. After that, all parts have been assembled, sewed, and finally finished with oil.

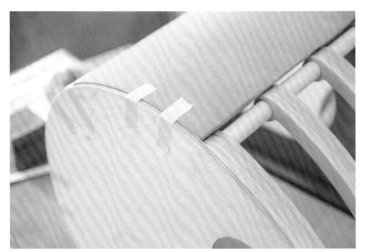

Knot Cushions

AGENCY /
Knots Studio

DESIGN /
Neta Tesler

PHOTOGRAPHY /
Ami Tesler

Knots Studio specializes in home décor products like sitting cushions, decorative cushions, and stools. All products utilize a unique tying technique which makes these pieces beautiful and functional. With the studio situated along the Mediterranean shore, their designs correspond with the aesthetics of the sea and the city lifestyle.

The pop color and texture of the sitting cushions contribute to interesting living room conversations.

MATERIAL

The cushions are made of a stiff-foam filling and upholstery material, making the pieces strong and durable.

CREATIVE

Knots Studio's artistic direction is influenced by functionality and creativity. The cushions are to add functional design and art to living space.

MAKING

The knot cushions utilize a unique lying technique. No fastens are needed.

LIGHTING

This chapter contains a wide range of indoor lights in various styles, unique materials, and fresh colors, including pendant lights, wall lights, floor lamps, and table lamps. The projects focus on ways to improve not only the visual shape of lighting devices, but also the quality and efficiency of lighting products.

Trans-Lamp

AGENCY /
KAIRI EGUCHI DESIGN

DESIGN /
Kairi Eguchi, Enya Hou

MANUFACTURE /
Brio Inc.

PHOTOGRAPHY /
Enya Hou

An experimental series that was designed based on the idea of applying theoretical mathematic calculation on standard products to form new products. When the products were being placed in the same space, they naturally linked to one and another, and added a graceful rhythm to the space. The lamps lighted a room or atmosphere gently with a shade covering the light source and controlling the glare. By shifting the heights to specific levels while preserving the volume of the frustum of cone, the designers presented a new series of lighting equipments that allowed the user's body to feel the same voluminous whilst changing the lamp's style depending on the usage.

MATERIAL

The frame was made of Japanese ash wood. The lampshade was made of Japanese paper and resin's core material.

MAKING

The frame was cut by machine and finished with oil. The lampshade involved paper pasting.

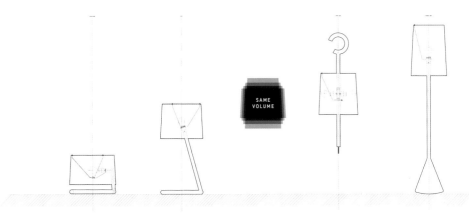

It was all about the idea of applying theoretical mathematic calculation to standard products to form new products. Also it was a combination of traditional material and craftsmanship with modern style design.

Du Côté de Chez Vous—Drôles d'Oiseaux

AGENCY /
Fritsch-Durisotti

Together with the armchair and ottoman featured in the chapter of furniture, the floor lamp and clothes rack are part of the series of "Drôles d'Oiseaux," which means "funny birds" in French. The projects have been presented at the design community event "Du Côté de Chez Vous." In this series, Fritsch-Durisotti has combined the traditional knitting craft with the high-end 3D printing technique. Each product is given a name corresponding a type of bird. The lamp is called "pullet," and the clothes rack "lark."

MATERIAL

Wood, wicker, and synthetic fiber are the main material.

CREATIVE

The projects explores the possibilities of different materials and crafts.

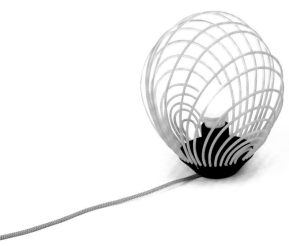

MAKING

Wickers are knitted to form the lampshade. The socket holder and connecting joints are manufactured by 3D printing technique.

Balancer

AGENCY /
YUUE

DESIGN /
Weng Xinyu

CLIENT /
Northern Lighting

Balancer is a showstopper in both function and form. Expertly crafted in black, powder-coated steel, this floor lamp offers a stunning combination of light, geometry, and style. Formed by clean, architectural lines, and classic geometrical shapes, Balancer is uniquely interactive.

At the turn of a swivel key, the shade levers upwards to cast light over the surroundings, or pivots downwards to direct it towards the floor. Balancer's brightness is both diffuse and direct, creating a careful balance of atmosphere and ambient light.

CREATIVE

As a rational solution for the counterbalancing mechanism, the curve and the knob also give the lamp a unique visual character.

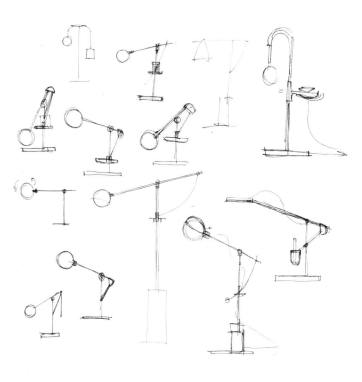

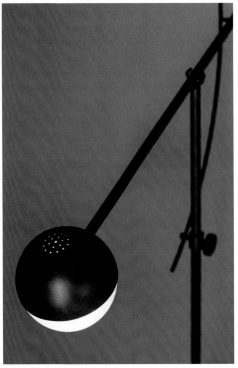

MATERIAL

Steel is the fundamental material of this design.

MAKING

From the beginning, metal models are made in 1:1 scale in a Berlin workshop to test the mechanism. The models turn out to be just perfect in both form and function. They are powder coated and fixed onto the bases. The spherical lampshades are CNC milled plastic to imitate the texture of metal and glass.

STRESS

DESIGN /
Ohad Benit

PHOTOGRAPHY /
Itay Benit

The term denotes a sense of strain, caused by imbalance. Ohad Benit sees himself at the taut boundary between himself and the world. Drawing inspiration from his feeling, he feels the light; reads its implications, expression, and role; and searches its existential, infinite, and quotidian presence inside of him. The materials, glass and brass, also reach their boundaries—two different forms run into and adjust to each other. The glass is hard and brittle, while the brass tough and elastic. The fluid glass is inflated manually through the brass rod—each lamp stands alone, different from its predecessor.

MATERIAL

Brass and glass are the main materials.

CREATIVE

The shape of glass is unique like the soap bubbles, both real and imaginary.

MAKING

Ohad made the shape of the brass in his studio by hand. With the brass shape ready, he went to his friend, a glass blower, and asked him to blow the glass in freestyle.

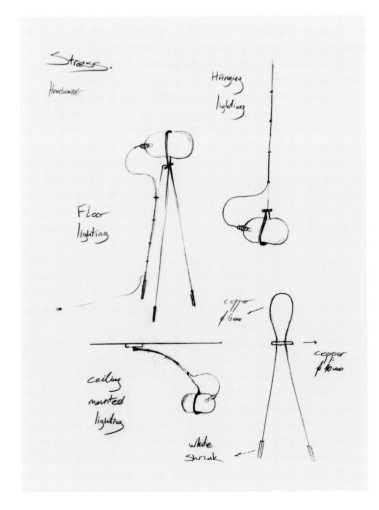

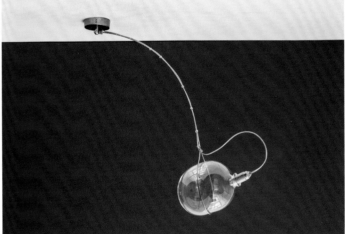

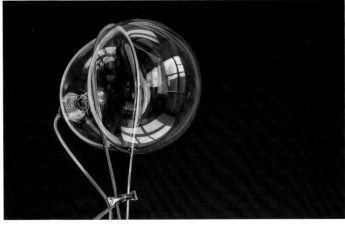

Chimney Light Series

AGENCY /
SWNA

DESIGN /
Sukwoo Lee

The Chimney Lighting resembles a form of simplified chimney, which emits warm and ambient light over Lycra, a fabric with elasticity. The series can be used as both floor lamp or a pendant, depending on the user's needs.

MATERIAL

The lighting is made of Lycra fabric, metal, and wood.

MAKING

The metal is shaped by hand. Wood is processed using CNC woodworking machine.

CREATIVE

The simple lines highlight the oval shape of the lightings. The light filters through the well-chosen white fabric, giving out a warm, dreamy color.

The inspiration for the inMoov lamp came from the movements in nature such as blooming flowers and swimming jellyfish. The designer wanted to transfer this fascinating movement into a living space.

inMoov

AGENCY /
Studio Lieven

DESIGN /
Nina Lieven

PHOTOGRAPHY /
**Simon Vollmeyer,
Nina Lieven,
James Wendlinger**

The unique feature of this lamp is its ability to folds itself inside out. Through this movement of the lampshade, it is possible to regulate the intensity and direction of the light. The fully opened lamp creates a soft light directed to the ceiling. The folded lamp creates more focused and warm light that illuminates the space underneath.

The movement can be adjusted by hand based on the user's individual needs. For the body of the lamp, the designer drew inspiration from the Invertible Cube of Paul Schatz and invented the Invertible Disc that could fold itself in and out.

Materials of the white lamp are textile, wood, steal, brass, and LED lights. Materials of the black lamp are textile, wood, carbon, PVC, and LED lights.

MAKING

The lamps are assembled by hand in Berlin.

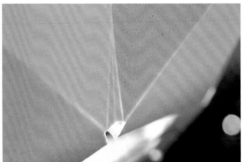

Whale

DESIGN /
Jaejin Lee

PHOTOGRAPHY /
Jaejin Lee

The lamp featured the shape of a white whale, known as the largest living creature on Earth. Pieces of wood were put together to form the whale frame. Through the frame, the user can see the light bulb. When the light was on, it would cast a shadow of whale on the wall. It can be used as a table lamp or a pendant.

MATERIAL

Birch plywood was used as a structural material.

CREATIVE

Creating the frame of the lamp was like playing with blocks. The product was designed to be functional and fun.

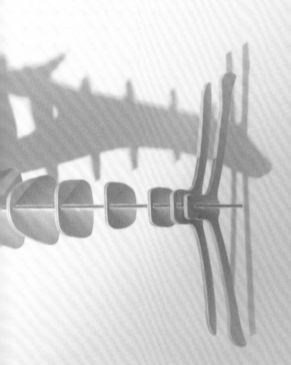

MAKING

Before starting the real project, the designer has run through a set of preparations from sketching, three-dimensional modeling, structure calculation. After all these were done, he created the floor plan, cut the wood by using CNC machine, assembled each part accordingly, and finally finished the frame with oil.

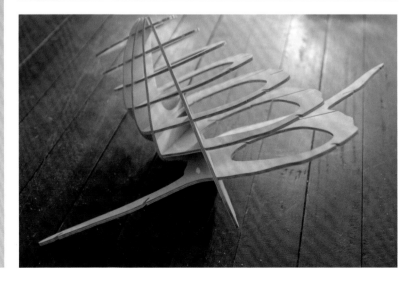

Bamboo Lights Layers

AGENCY /
Daphna Laurens

CLIENT /
Duc Phong

PHOTOGRAPHY /
Duc Phong

"Layers" is a set of lamps. Each lamp has three different layers of bamboo shapes with different types bamboo weavings. The bamboo weavings are made by a Vietnamese company Duc Phong specialized in bamboo knitting. In this way the company can show their expertise in different types of bamboo weaving craft.

MATERIAL

Bamboo veneer is the fundamental material.

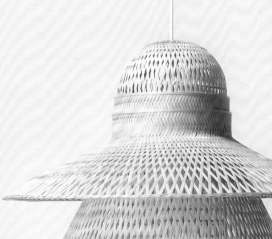

MAKING

Traditional bamboo weaving techniques are used to create the lamp shades.

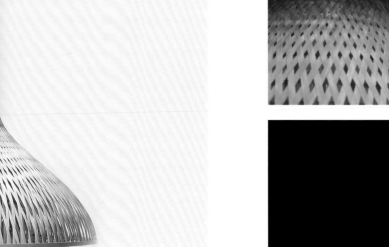

CREATIVE

The designer
attempted to
reintroduce traditional
craftsmanship
into contemporary
furniture making.

"/" Lamp

AGENCY /
Dragos Motica Studio

When an object is designed? When an object is precious, particular? What is broken and what is new? What means the result of a mechanical intervention (more or less violent on an object)? What is an vulgarized object?

"/" Lamp is an object that gives the chance of choice—a subjective and personal choice. It is an object at the middle of two opposite states. Intervention or non-intervention places it in one of them. The materials used for building the lamp are inspired by the industrial facilities, by the construction sites: concrete, reinforcing wire, rope climbing, spool for high voltage wires.

MATERIAL

Reinforced concrete, cork, LED, and birch plywood are chosen for this project. Concrete is the entire esthetic of the lamp. The cork inside is meant to protect the LED lights if the user chooses to break it.

CREATIVE

The main intent of this object was to provoke the user and to establish a personal relationship between the lamp and its end user, making it more "valuable" to the user. Giving the possibility to choose between breaking it or leaving it intact is meant to establish the personal, powerful relation.

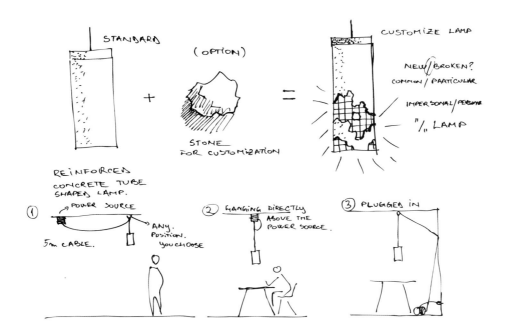

STANDARD   (OPTION)

+

STONE
FOR CUSTOMIZATION

=

CUSTOMIZE LAMP

NEW / BROKEN?
COMMON / PARTICULAR

IMPERSONAL / PERSONAL

" " LAMP

REINFORCED
CONCRETE TUBE
SHAPED LAMP.

① → POWER SOURCE

5m CABLE.

→ ANY.
POSITION.
YOU CHOOSE

② HANGING DIRECTLY ABOVE THE POWER SOURCE.

③ PLUGGED IN

The body for the lamp is produced by pouring reinforced concrete (colored, if needed) into a silicone mould. The concrete shape is then air dried and polished until it reaches a smooth exterior. The inside core is a round shaped cork, cut on a CNC machine, and inserted into the concrete shape.

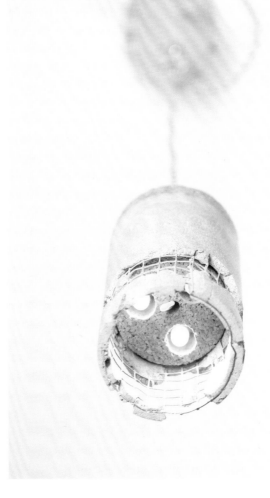

SVETOCH

DESIGN /
Anastasiya Koshcheeva

Svetoch is a set of birch bark lamps. The concept of Svetoch Lamp is based on a traditional glue-free craft method of joining birch bark parts together, combining it with a laser-cut structure and celebrating the material. The lamp produces a very soft and diffused light, playing with shadows and making every room cozy. There are two sizes available for the lamp: one is 150mm in depth, 520mm in height; the other 250mm in depth, 200mm in height.

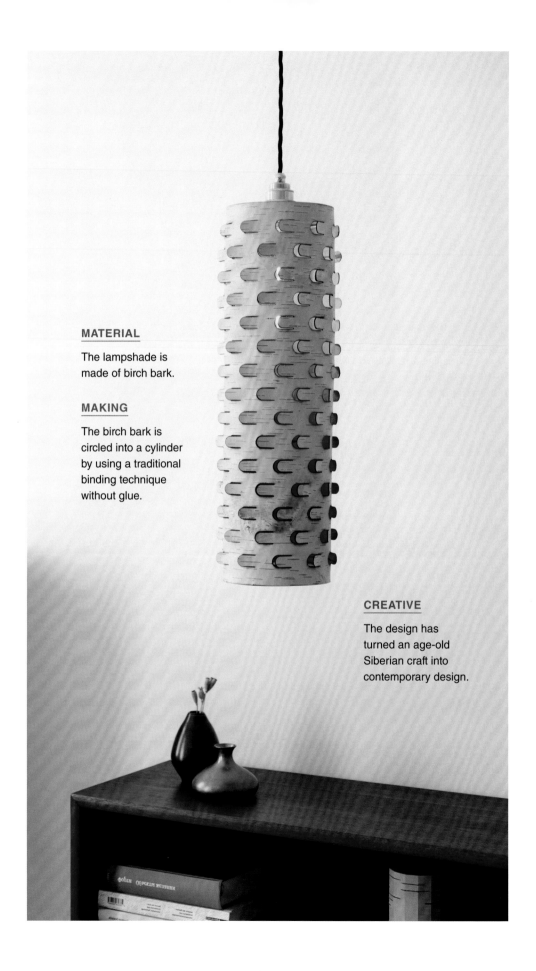

MATERIAL

The lampshade is made of birch bark.

MAKING

The birch bark is circled into a cylinder by using a traditional binding technique without glue.

CREATIVE

The design has turned an age-old Siberian craft into contemporary design.

MATERIAL

Steel and light bulbs
are the fundamental
materials.

MAKING

The steel are cut
using laser and
shaped into a
desirable frame.

U32-1

AGENCY /
SHIFT

CLIENT /
LampsLite

SHIFT introduces a line of lighting
for lamp manufacturer LampsLite.
The pendants are constructed
entirely from metal. U32-1 explores
the concept of modern lighting,
taking heavily after contemporary
urban trends, particularly the
tension and structure of the modern
city landscape. Composed of two
icosahedral geometries (a polyhedron
with 20 faces), the lamp is suspended
inside an angular wire frame,
presenting a distinct angular dialogue
between surface and frame.

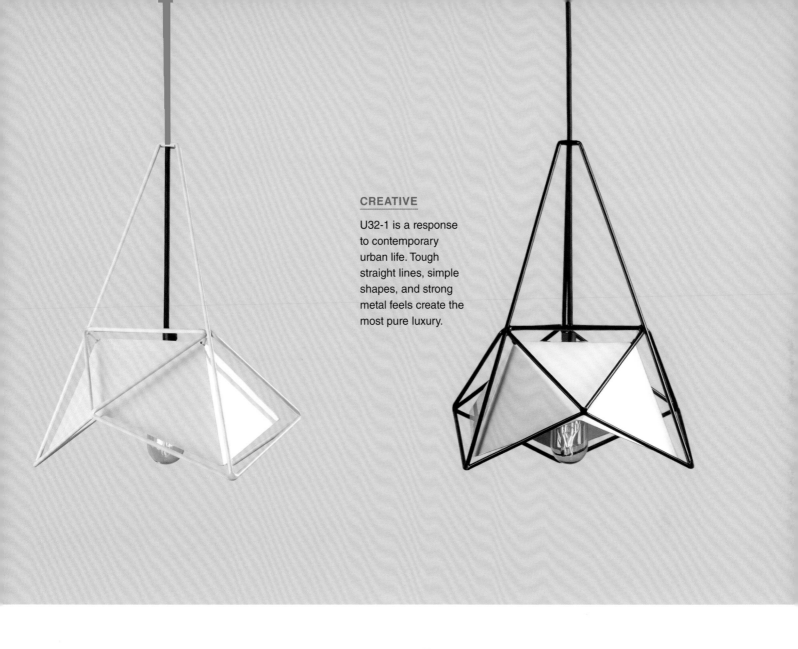

CREATIVE

U32-1 is a response to contemporary urban life. Tough straight lines, simple shapes, and strong metal feels create the most pure luxury.

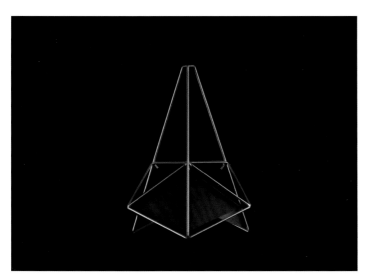

Light Container

DESIGN /
Martín Azúa

Light Container presents a mass of light inside a metallic basket that seems floating. Light is immaterial, but at the same time lamps are also objects. In this case, light is treated as something with weight and volume.

The lamps are made in three different sizes that can be hung individually or in groups of two. The glass diffuser generates a nice warm dim light with soft shadows, suitable for restaurant tables, counters, receptions, meeting and working tables. Its sculptural character allows the personalization of singular halls, stairwells.

MATERIAL

Metal is used to create the frame of the lamp.

CREATIVE

The lamps can double as container and a good piece of decorative object.

MAKING

The metal is shaped into a basket.

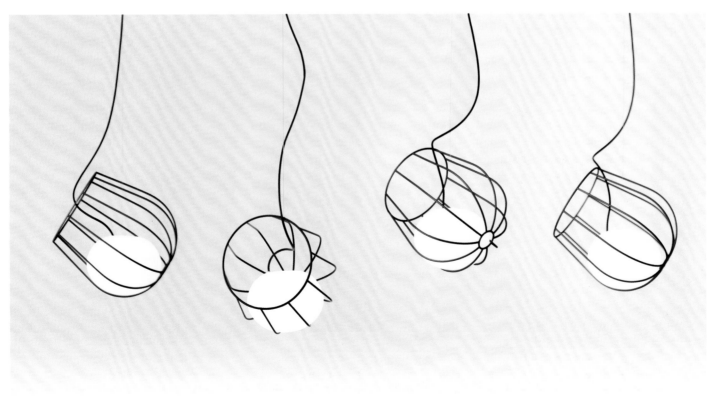

N LAMP

DESIGN /
Dragos Motica Studio

PRODUCTION /
Ubikubi

N Lamp's design was inspired by the traditional water pumps that one can find in the rural areas of Romania. The lamp is comprised of a metallic horizontal tube attached perpendicularly on a vertical one. At the shorter end of the horizontal structure, a marble counterweight is placed to hold the balance. The connection between the two structures is made via a chromed metallic ball which allows an almost 360 degrees rotary move of the lamp's arm.

The marble base holds the entire weight of the structure and has an integrated light switch. The light switch is the intriguing and central element of the lamp. By moving the metallic sphere from one indentation to the other, the light is turn on or off. The N lamp offers a warm, glare-free light, by using LED technology.

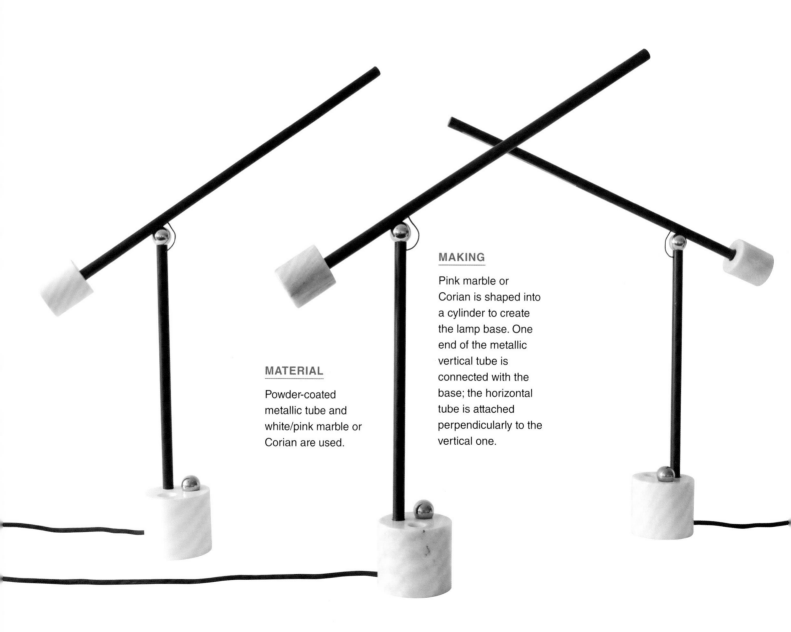

MATERIAL

Powder-coated metallic tube and white/pink marble or Corian are used.

MAKING

Pink marble or Corian is shaped into a cylinder to create the lamp base. One end of the metallic vertical tube is connected with the base; the horizontal tube is attached perpendicularly to the vertical one.

CREATIVE

The user experience is transformed, by allowing the person to manipulate the sphere to participate in "the creation of light." The invisible switch works by placing in the marble base an inductive sensor which functions in the same way as electric stoves do.

ON Lamp:
On Polar Series

AGENCY /
ilsangisang

DESIGN /
Jong-su Kim

ON Lamp is a set of table LED lamps whose lampshades take the shape of endangered polar animals: polar bear, emperor penguin, blonde fur seal, snowy owl, and white fox. Using DC 5V by connecting with USB, it has an excellent energy consumption ratio. Its lampshade is made of recyclable material, which means that it is an environment friendly LED lamp. This series of lampshades tell the users stories of the endangered environment, helping them realize the importance and urgency of environmental protection.

MATERIAL

PP, LED, wood, iron, and magnet are used. The legs of the LED base are made of ash wood to add natural touch.

MAKING

The DIY lampshade is designed based on creative structural packaging, which has a built-in magnet plate. The plate can be attached to the LED base station with a built-in iron plate.

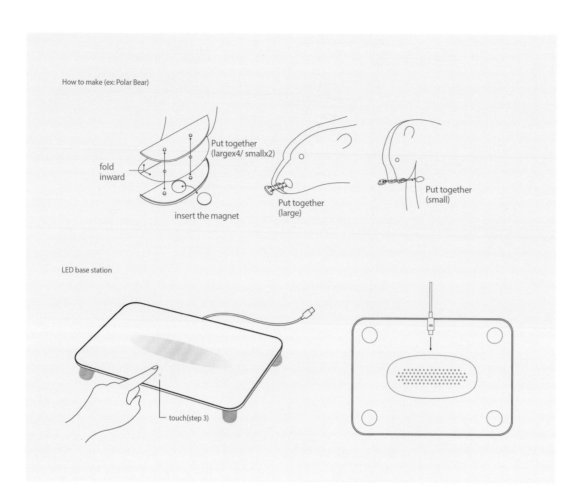

How to make (ex: Polar Bear)

fold inward

insert the magnet

Put together (largex4/ smallx2)

Put together (large)

Put together (small)

LED base station

touch(step 3)

CREATIVE

The series is a
new concept of a
standing-type lamp
for homes with which
consumers may
change to their liking.

Nuvola Light

DESIGN /
Malika Novi

Nuvola Light is a conceptual design of lamp, applying the use of LED technology. The small lamp is covered by soft substrate on which pieces of laser-cut polycarbonate are glued.

When the lamp is on, it gives out soft light, adding some sort of peaceful atmosphere to the space. The lamp has been made manually.

CREATIVE

The lamp is made of multiple layers of materials, yet it can be achieved easily by hand.

MATERIAL

Fabric, polycarbonate, and LED lights are used in this project.

MAKING

The lamp prototype was made from light strips that were attached to a padded base and covered by soft substrate fabric. The polycarbonate was cut into prismatic pieces using laser. The pieces were glued manually on the fabric.

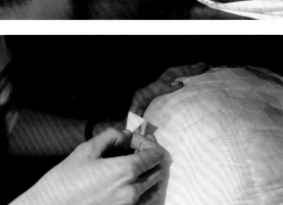

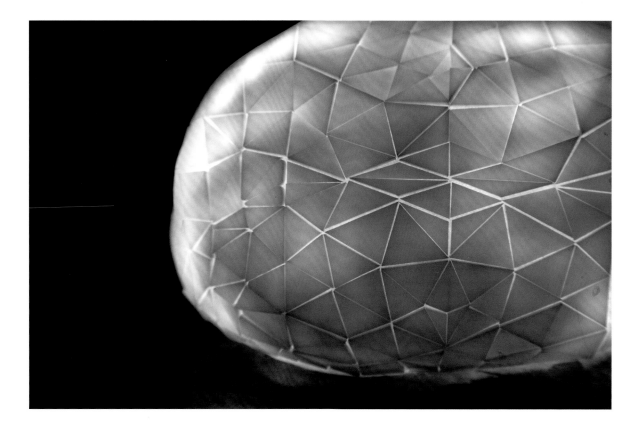

MATERIAL

Sand is the
fundamental material.

Sand Light

AGENCY /
alien and monkey

Sand Light is part of alien and monkey's "Sand Made Project," a series of designs that continue to explore this new sustainable material, including Sand Packaging and Sand Furniture. The design concept stems from the Freudian idea that the loss of objects awakens memories and emotions within their owner. A product's physical evolution caused by time and its owner's mishaps will create deeper emotional bonds between them. Ephemeral in

essence, the Sand lamp can last for a long period of time, and slowly crumble back to dust at the end of their lives, leaving behind just grains of sand and other minerals that are harmless to the environment.

Sand Light is available in three natural colors, white, nude, and black. Each light comes with a customized brass holder. It can be used as self-supporting table light or strung in groups as ceiling light.

MAKING

Employing a traditional process and a touch of alchemy, particles of sand are shaped and formed into objects. By varying the specifics of the process, like pressure, temperature, percentage of added minerals, different properties of longevity and strength can be developed so as to modify the material to suit different applications.

CREATIVE

The idea behind is to make products that can last for a long period of time and do no harm to the environment.

Bento

AGENCY /
YUUE

DESIGN /
Weng Xinyu

Bento is an interactive portable lamp. To turn on the lamp is as intuitive as pulling the band on the top. The light gently goes on automatically. Reversing the action will turn off the lamp. The structure is possible thanks to the extendable pole and a flexible silicone lampshade. The cylinder chamber even doubles as storage for small objects. Bento can be used either on the desk, or beside the bed; either indoors, or outdoors. The built-in rechargeable batteries make sure that light is always by your side!

MATERIAL

The main materials are plastic, aluminum, and silicone.

MAKING

YUUE was working very closely with factories to produce various parts: retractable tubes, PCB with sensors and battery, LED and silicone lampshade. The lamp has to be assembled and disassembled thousands of times until the design is finalized.

CREATIVE

Bento is a portable lamp with intuitive and fun user experience, just like opening a lunch box. Hidden inside the adorable Bento box is the genius technology and engineering of mechanism, material, and electronics.

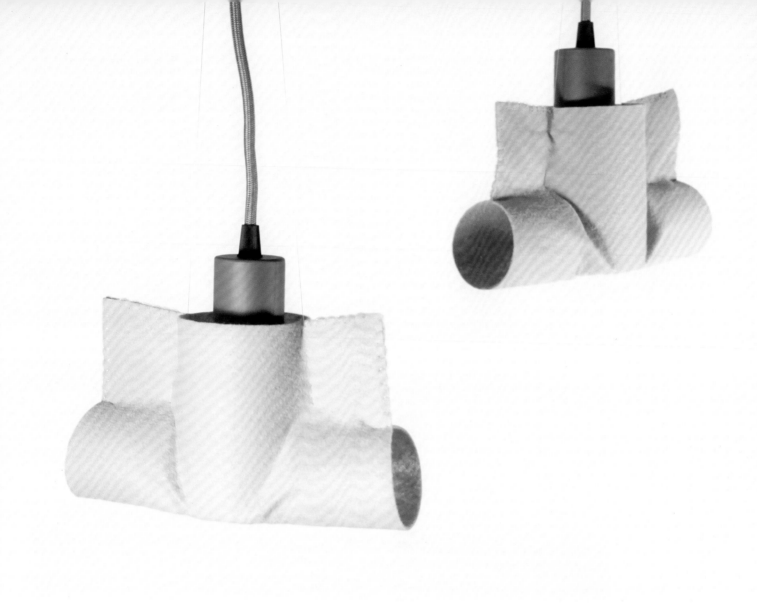

Wrinkle

DESIGN /
Ken Chen

Through investigating creative ways to collect, experiment, and utilize discarded material, Ken Chen created a series of felt pendant light.

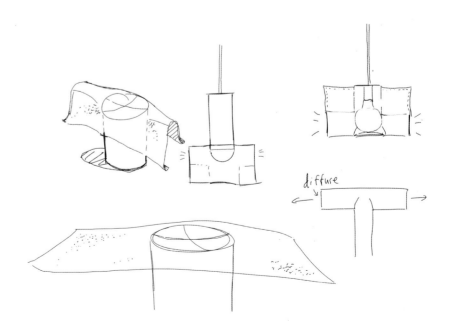

diffuse

MATERIAL

Felt and fishing line are used for the series.

MAKING

The making process involves stiffening the materials to form a simple mold of the light.

CREATIVE

It is a new way to make use of the waste material.

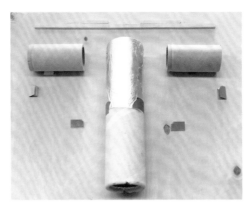

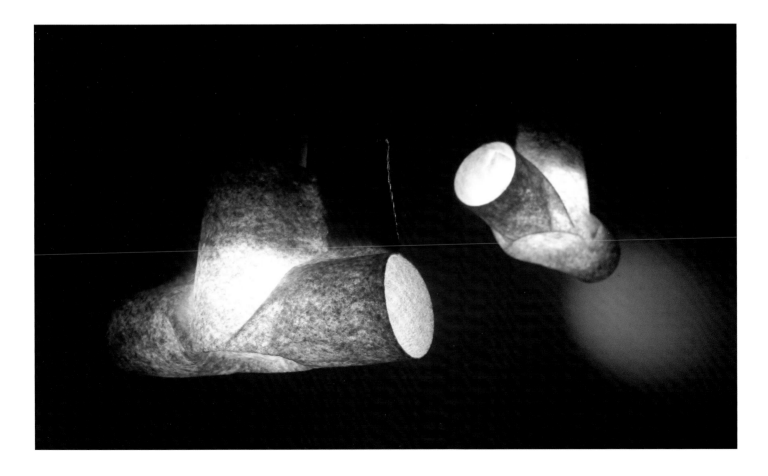

Monolith Light

DESIGN /
Shira Keret

CLIENT /
ReDesign **Magazine for Regba**

PHOTOGRAPHY /
Daniel Shechter

For this project, Shira Keret teamed up with *ReDesign* Magazine to create Monolith Light—a series of light fixtures, based on the same methodology and esthetics of the original Monolith series of marble objects. Monolith Light is a series of wall mounted light fixtures. Each of them is unique in its mixture of ridges and blend of colors.

The flat discs that comprise the lamps are crafted from thinly sliced Corian blocks. The use of Corian, a polymer based solid surface material, has enabled the seamless blending of colors and textures in a single slab. Each disc is held in place by brass prongs, which is fixed to the base of the lamp without damaging its surface.

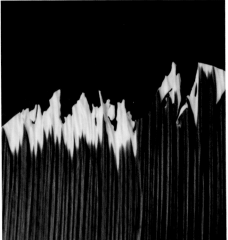

MATERIAL

Corian blocks, brass, and LED lights are used in this project.

MAKING

The blocks are first cut by water jet machine and then processed by hand to create varied textures.

CREATIVE

The varied ridges and textures on the stone produce a color circle of varying hues.

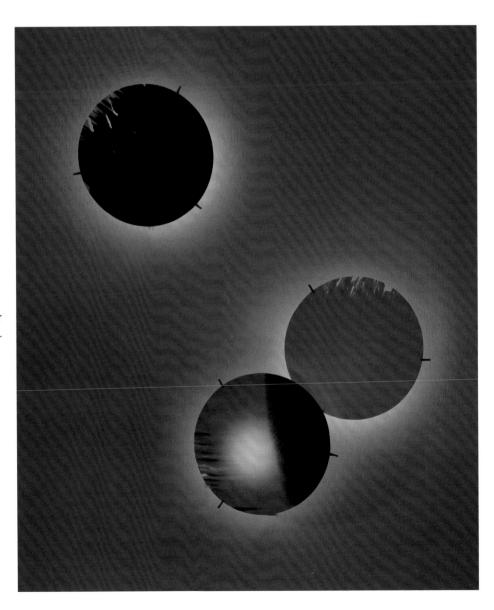

Stingray-Pendant Lamp

DESIGN /
Ankit Tatiya

The goal of this project was to design a product drawing inspiration from nature. Ankit Tatiya chose stingray as the inspiration. Stingrays are fascinating creatures—they float and fly in the oceans just like birds spreading their wings and soaring in the sky. Starry dots on the back of a stingray look enchanting.

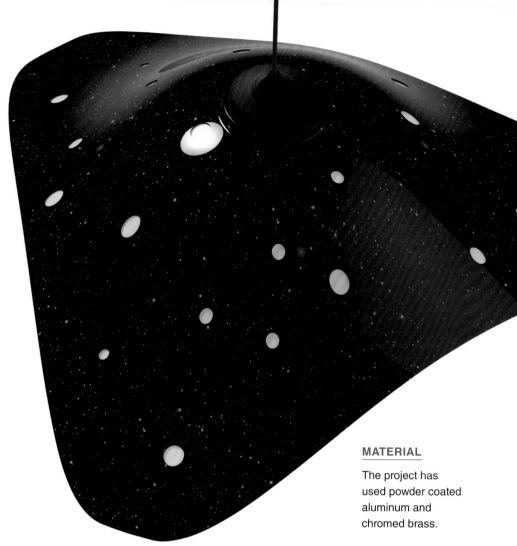

MAKING

The aluminum is spun as lampshade. Each part is designed, decorated, and drilled by the hands of skilled designers and craftsmen.

CREATIVE

Inspired by nature, the pendant lamp carries the beauty of the sea creature, stingray.

MATERIAL

The project has used powder coated aluminum and chromed brass.

Jurassic Light 117

AGENCY /
Studio Dessuant Bone

PHOTOGRAPHY /
Studio Dessuant Bone

For Another Country's 5th anniversary exhibition "The Dorset Series," during London Design Festival, Studio Dessuant Bone was invited to design a limited edition object inspired by the brands Dorset's origins.

Jurassic Light 117 is inspired by the Jurassic Coast's Durdle Door, an iconic landmark of the Dorset coastline. The cylindrical negative space created by this arch has been interpreted to create the simple shape that forms the light. Jurassic Light 117 employs Portland stone that carries impressions of fossils from the Dorset area—acting as a constant reminder of the origins of the design.

MATERIAL

The lamp base is made of Portland stone and brass.

MAKING

The Portland stone is cut and shaped into a cylinder which is used as the lamp base.

CREATIVE

The gray stone and golden brass work perfectly and render the lamp a luxurious feeling.

Antumbra Lamp

AGENCY /
Monitillo Marmi

DESIGN /
Magnus Long Design Studio

Antumbra is a touch-dimmable marble table lamp. Polished black marquina marble is used for the front stone to occlude light; matt-finished white carrara marble is used to reflect and diffuse light off of the larger back stone, creating a glowing diffused light which can be dimmed or increased by touching and holding the marble. As the front marble slab occludes the light source, an effect similar to an annular eclipse is seen from the front, specially known as the "antumbra" (before shadow), where the front opaque object appears completely in silhouette with a halo of light surrounding it. When the lamp is turned off, the object reverts to a simple decoration of standing stones in black and white marble.

CREATIVE

The design follows ancient sculptors' observations on white marble glowing in light due to its ability to create diffuse reflections—where light actually enters the surface of the marble before being scattered and diffused by the top layer of crystals. The designer wanted to play on this physical property by using white marble as a reflector and diffuser, and black marble as a "mask" for the light source.

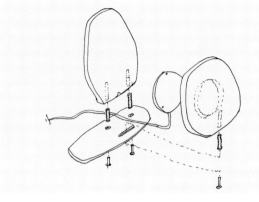

The marble stones are set onto a powder-coated steel base and the cable discreetly exits at the back of the lamp. An internal touch-sensitive switch within the front stone allows the light-intensity to be increased or decreased by touching and holding the stone.

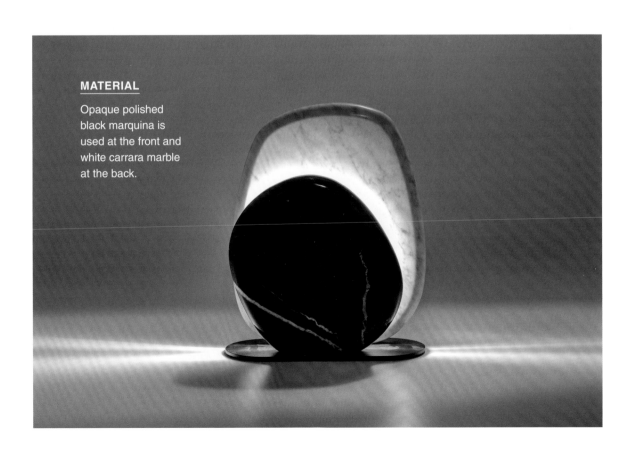

MATERIAL

Opaque polished black marquina is used at the front and white carrara marble at the back.

Onddo Lamp

AGENCY /
Iratzoki Lizaso

CLIENT /
Goiko

PHOTOGRAPHY /
Mito

Onddo is a nomad lamp made from kiln-fired, enamelled terracotta. The source of light comes from LEDs fitted into the upper part of the lamp which reflects off the enamel to create a softly colored light.

CREATIVE

The designers wanted to transform the technical working with terracotta into a new type of object.

MATERIAL

The lampshade is made of Terracotta. The light bulb type is LED.

MAKING

The terracotta lampshade is made on a wheel.

Wood Mosaic: Lighting

AGENCY /
KAIRI EGUCHI DESIGN

DESIGN /
Kairi Eguchi, Enya Hou

MANUFACTURE /
Brio Inc.

PHOTOGRAPHY /
Manabu Sato

"Beautiful Remnants—Valuing the beauty of remnants over lumber." The wood that the designers use as material is lumbered. In the manufacturing process of furniture, there are some parts left out: the remnants. Even though they are harvested from the same tree, remnants are marked as low-value from the start. The designers' intention was to create something beautiful out of these remnants—something more beautiful than being made out of lumber. Their thoughts went into the hopes of raising the value of remnants, leading to a new door for an environmental-friendly product making.

This series consists of furniture and lighting, all developed under the concept of "Remnants is more beautiful than lumber." The smooth texture of the wood is also luxurious, almost like a carved stone, creating a beautiful atmosphere.

MATERIAL

The lampshade is made of cedar chip and urethane. The lamp base is of beech wood. The frame is constructed mainly with steel. The paint used is emulsion in consideration of the environment.

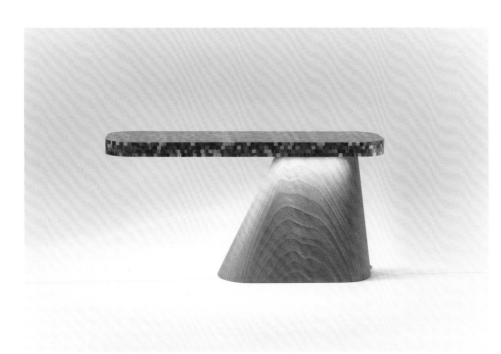

CREATIVE

It is all about the idea of valuing the beauty of remnants over lumber. The designers believe in nature beauty. Other than that, the lamp is ultra lightweight, which is easy to lift and tends to have lower transportation costs.

MAKING

The whole series was made out of remnants of Japanese cedar in block shapes, which then was put together in mosaic. The top board run through a process of cutting, pasting, compressing, and finishing coating. Steel was cut using laser to form the frame of the lamp.

Matter Lamp

AGENCY /
SHIFT

Matter can ultimately be converted into energy. This was Shift's main premise when designing the Matter lamp—a study on the relation and states of matter as it can be changed from one form to another. Matter in the form of positrons and electrons can be changed into photons, hence the Matter lamp's solid and light elements. Made from black concrete disks that intersect with wooden structures, the Matter lamp continues Shift's experimentation with concrete's peculiar aesthetics while generating a spherical shape and structure that allude to the design's scientific foundation.

MATERIAL

The lamp is made of walnut wood and concrete.

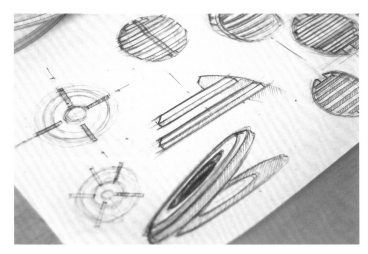

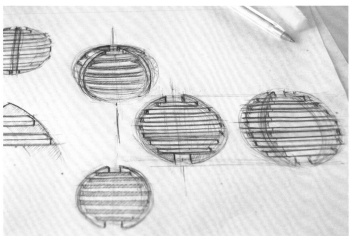

MAKING

The lampshade is made by casting concrete into molds. The wood is cut using CNC cutting machine.

CREATIVE

Its manufacturing brings together the old and new, by combining industrial craftsmanship and CNC precision.

Outsiders

AGENCY /
Panter&Tourron

PHOTOGRAPHY /
Jagoda Wisniewska

From a long-lasting fascination for fire comes a series of outdoor oil lamps and lanterns. Fire is a moving and living power that seems uncontrollable at first. It influences human environments and moods with its warmness and comforting qualities.

This project aims to challenge the concept of fire and design a series of objects that are grasping this uneasy force. A set of lantern, torches, candle holder, and a fire pit speak about man's passion for exploring the outdoors.

MATERIAL

The main materials are aluminum, brass, and wood.

MAKING

The process involves metal and wood spinning/embossing

CREATIVE

The project explores the ways of storing fire.

Ripple

DESIGN /
Ken Chen

ART DIRECTION /
Tom Weis

Ripple is a table lamp derived from woodworking techniques such as steam-bending and staves construction. It is made of ash wood with a concrete base. While having the same curvature, the steam-bent staves revolve around a circle to shape a rhythmic form. The thin edges and top rim reveal a weightless impression.

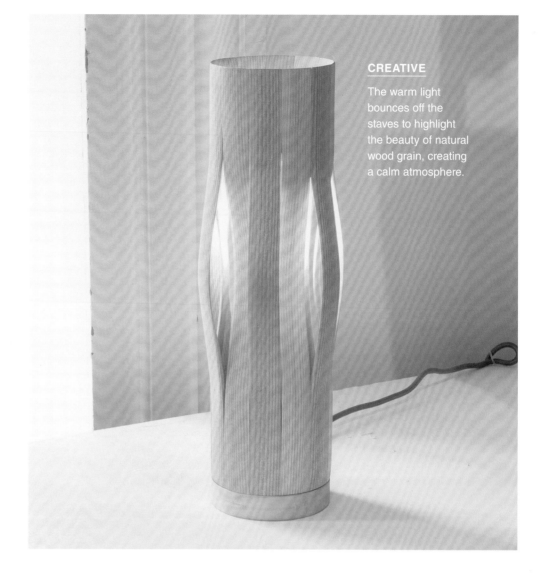

CREATIVE

The warm light bounces off the staves to highlight the beauty of natural wood grain, creating a calm atmosphere.

MATERIAL

Ash wood and concrete are used.

MAKING

The lampshade is processed with woodworking. The lamp base is made by casting concrete into a specific mold.

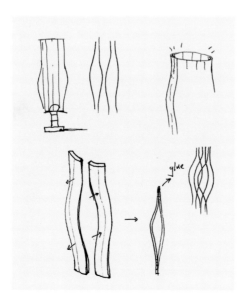

Unibody Lamp

DESIGN /
Julius Graupner

Unibody is a one piece lamp that is 3D printed and requires no making. The lamp has a thread that holds standard E27 socket. The pattern on the body is generated in grasshopper.

CREATIVE

The lamp is created using 3D printing technique.

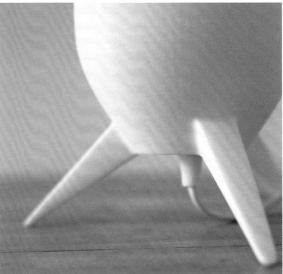

MATERIAL

Nylon is the raw material of the lamp.

MAKING

Nylon is sintered by using selective laser sintering (SLS) technique. During sintering, particles of the nylon are bound together to create a solid structure.

Lufa Series: Lamp

DESIGN /
Fernando Laposse

Loofah is the fruit from a tropical vine that is related to pumpkins and cucumbers, which grows vertically attaching itself to trees. Once this fruit matures, it is then dried and harvested, leaving a xylem of fibers behind, which is mainly used for scrubbing. Fernando Laposse has come up with Lufa Series to exploit one or several of the qualities of this material, like lightness, translucency, heat insulation, texture, and shock absorption, etc. This lamp is one of the objects in this series.

MATERIAL

The lamp stand is made of wood. The lampshade is made of loofah fibers.

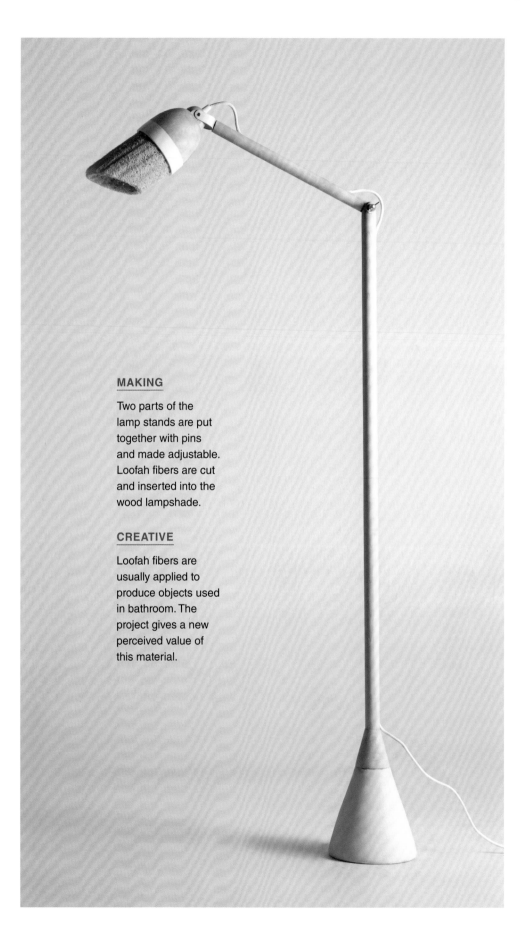

MAKING

Two parts of the lamp stands are put together with pins and made adjustable. Loofah fibers are cut and inserted into the wood lampshade.

CREATIVE

Loofah fibers are usually applied to produce objects used in bathroom. The project gives a new perceived value of this material.

ACCESSORIES

Home, office or decorative accessories in good design and quality can liven up one's living space. This chapter includes outstanding accessories designs ranging from baskets to tableware, stationery, vases, carpets, decorative objects—every design can add style and utility to space in one way or another.

Romantic Adventure

AGENCY /
Panter&Tourron

PHOTOGRAPHY /
Jagoda Wisniewska

Adventure Romantique is a picnic backpack inspired by travels, adventures, and outdoor lifestyle. It stands for the will to share unique moments and relationships. The use of skin color leather and rattan represents the freshness of first warm seasons of the year, where people forget the cold winter and leave for new adventures.

The project was designed for the exhibition Arts & Crafts & Design: Time according to ECAL and Swiss Craftsmen presented by Vacheron Constantin, curated by Studio Formafantasma, which took place during the Milan Design Week 2015. The final project was realized in collaboration with the Swiss saddler Patricia Rochat.

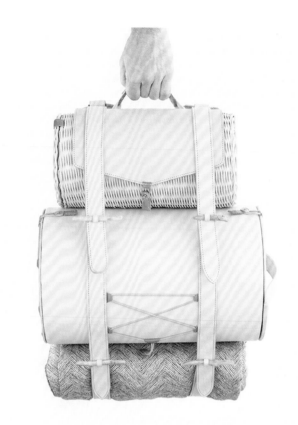

MATERIAL

The product is mainly made of leather.

MAKING

The leather is sewed and molded by the Swiss craftsman.

CREATIVE

Nowadays luxury represents the research for powerful experiences rather than the desire to possess the actual object.

Nomadic Life

AGENCY /
Gerardo Osio

DESIGN /
Gerardo Sandoval Osio

ART DIRECTION /
Kentaro Yamamoto, Yoshito Nakano

Created with the assistance from JICA and the Kyoto Institute of Technology, Nomadic Life is a selection of objects, inspired by Japanese culture and traditional crafts. The case can be carried from a living place to another, making it easy to create a familiar space anywhere. This project aims to present how

Japanese culture and traditional crafts can solve the problems of shrinking living spaces and nomadic lifestyle by lending simplicity, practicability, and essence of Japan's two main religious philosophies—Buddhism and Shinto—to contemporary living phenomena.

CREATIVE

This project is inspired by Buddhist and Shinto religions, especially the essentials of wellbeing advocated by the two religions. The project is a homage to simplicity, appreciation for the impermanent, and the reconnection with nature.

MATERIAL

Nomadic Life has the purpose to create a space with simple objects that reminds the user of home. The product is made from natural materials: copper, wood, leather, straw, cotton, and stone; the objects can tell a story as time goes by, creating a sense of belonging when they are used.

MAKING

This project was made in collaboration with six different Japanese traditional craft workshops. All the objects are hand made by the craftsmen in Kyoto, Fukui, and Okayama.

Magma Rug

DESIGN /
Martín Azúa

Martín Azúa has created Magma Rug in collaboration with craftswomen from Murcia. Esparto grass rugs are usually round or rectangular. The process of braiding and sewing the rugs is a rather repetitive activity usually done in teams of two or three women who talk and sing while they work. Without breaking their way of working, a series of rugs are made with forms that are quite different from the traditional ones. The rugs start from different centers which expand and finally generate an organic surface full of energy. The series presents rugs that have three, four, or five central circles in different sizes. Martín said that the rug reminds him of the feeling of expanding and spreading as liquid.

MAKING

The rug is made by craftswomen from the region of Murica. The craftswomen start from the center and generate circles by placing the esparto braid and sewing it.

CREATIVE

Reclaiming this type of craftsmanship for a contemporary product means an opportunity for the survival of a traditional profession, a local know-how.

MATERIAL

Esparto grass rugs are the main materials, which are 100% natural with a very particular smell and touch. The rug can be cleaned with a vacuum cleaner, a broom, or a brush.

The Palm Project

DESIGN /
Moisés Hernández

ASSISTANCE /
Fernanda Leal, Sandy Avellaneda

CLIENT /
Mexican Secretary Of Culture

Invited by the Secretary of Culture, Moisés Hernández and his team travelled to Tlamacazapa, Guerrero, a small town, where a variety of woven palm products are handcrafted. The objective was to generate new designs to reinforce the regional economic development through the commercialization of original objects. This project was developed with twenty craftswomen from Tlamacazapa. The project involved three concepts: the use of complementary materials, color, and a tribute to the palm—a precious material. These exercises are based on the techniques and typology that craftswomen already commercialize: baskets and bags.

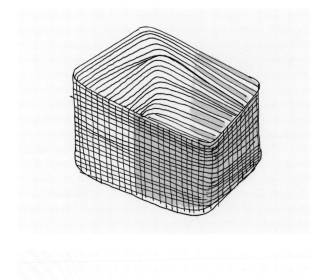

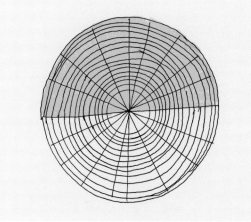

MATERIAL

The baskets and bags are made from palm, cooper, and cellulose.

MAKING

The products are all woven manually by traditional craftswomen using palm and cellulose.

CREATIVE

Traditional crafts are reinterpreted in modern design context.

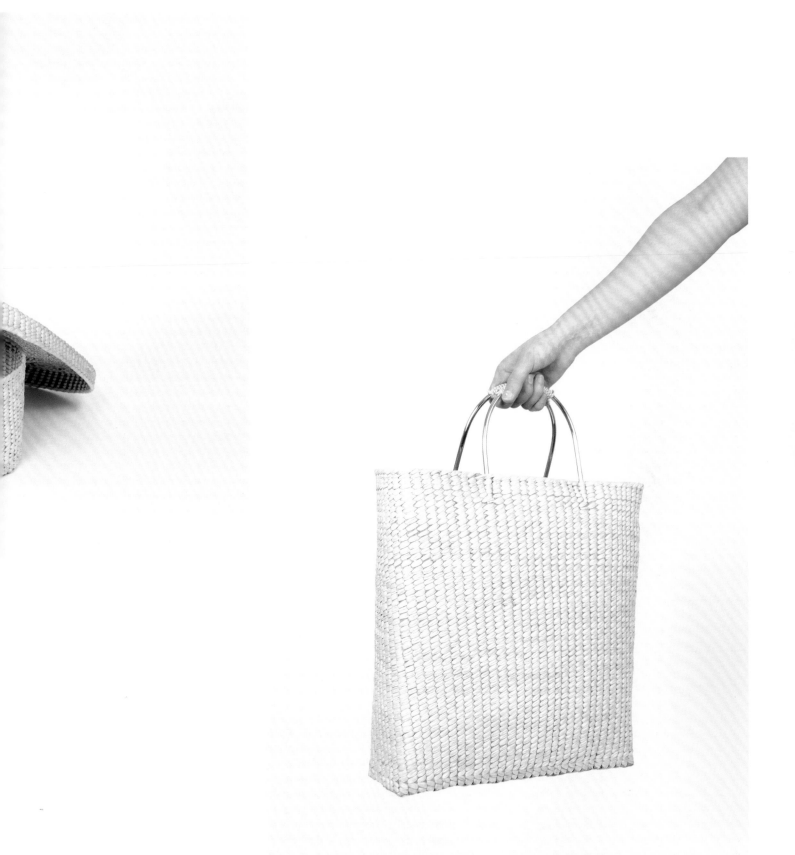

The users can imagine the movements of objects with the see-saw structure of the bookshelf.

ODDLY
Bookshelf

AGENCY /
Oddly Studio

DESIGN /
Youngmin Kang

PHOTOGRAPHY /
Youngmin Kang

This project started with the idea that household items would be able to add energy to many people if they were designed to function in a new structure, beyond the static and tedious vertical and horizontal structure. Traditional bookshelves are mostly designed in a vertical or horizontal structure. Youngmin wanted to design a fun, moving object beyond the existing structure. He spent two months trying to solve this problem and finally found a very good structure—stable and moving—a see-saw structure.

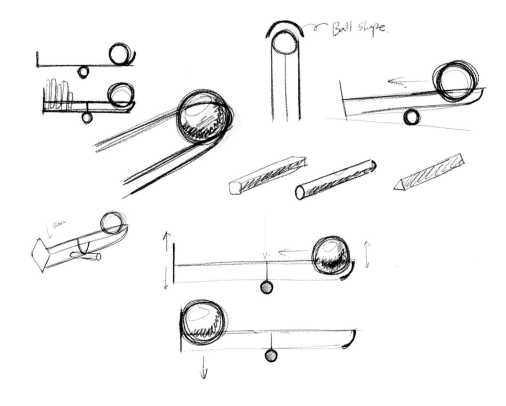

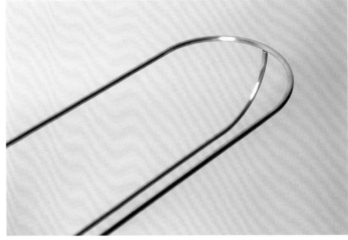

MATERIAL

The book shelf is largely made of two materials: brass and walnut wood. In the place where the book is placed, a square plate that matches the shape of the book is used. A metal rod is used as wire rod.

MAKING

Two methods of metal working were applied: bending and welding. Wood processing was done manually. Since it was not possible to make a wooden ball into a piece, a plate of appropriate thickness was piled up. The ball and rod were made using a wooden panel.

Burn Bowl

DESIGN /
Anna Gudmundsdottir

Anna Gudmundsdottir came up with this project in collaboration with Iceland Academy of the Arts. In the ever-accelerating pace of urban life, there is a general urge to slow down in order to fully appreciate experiences. This concept was inspired by primitive methods of cooking and crafting to engage people to embrace simple, outdoor pleasures such as tool making and cooking over an open fire. The wooden bottom can be transformed into a container through an activity of coal burning wood and hot stone cooking. It is an activity about putting focus on what is meaningful and fulfilling in life and strengthening human's relationship with nature.

MATERIAL

The bottom is made of locally produced Icelandic aspen wood, a type of heat resistant and lightweight wood, making the product easily portable. The top lid is made of basalt, one of the most common sub-volcanic rocks in Iceland. The metal parts are stainless steel and the strap is made from Icelandic reindeer leather.

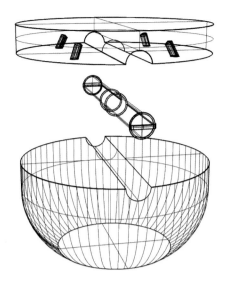

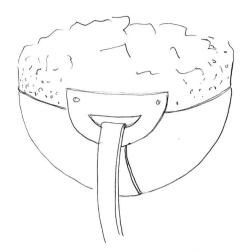

MAKING

The wood is processed by hand. The rock is sawed and drilled. The metal are welded while the leather is simply sewn together.

CREATIVE

This project is based on the concept of using fire as a tool to craft one's own natural cooking equipment out of wood.

Postures

DESIGN /
Carl Kleiner

MANUFACTURE /
Bloc Studios

PHOTOGRAPHY /
Carl Kleiner

Carl Kleiner designed the Posture in collaboration with Bloc Studios. The Postures vases originate from a photo series made by Carl as a personal project. The pictures portrait French tulips as levitating dancers, sometimes in group and sometimes alone. Through an enthusiastic Swiss student, the pictures found their way to Sara Ferron Cima, owner of a workshop and the student's teacher. From there, the actual products have been developed under the joint forces of designers from Sweden and Italy. The final products have been presented at Salone del mobile Milano 2017.

MATERIAL

The base is made of marble. The holder on top is made of brass.

MAKING

The developing process was a mix of sketches, computer generated renderings, wood blocks, and brass processing.

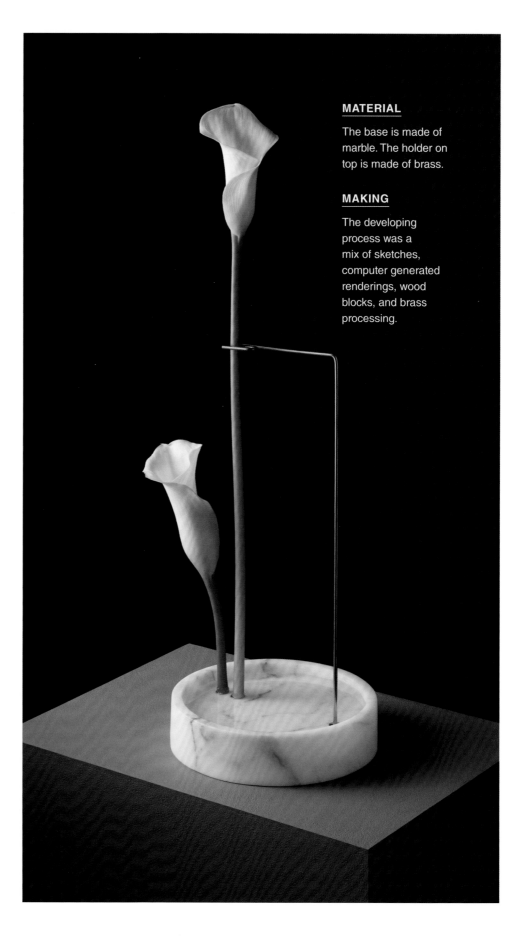

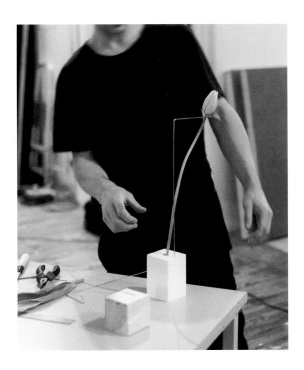

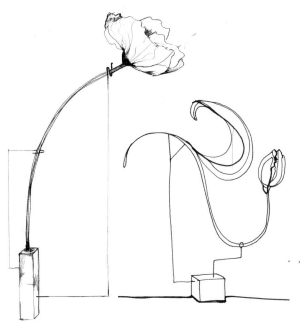

The aim was to translate the original photographs into a product that holds flowers for a period of time longer than a photo shoot. The biggest challenge was to ground the flower in the water yet keep the tension and floating feel from the arrangements in the photographs.

Disguise

AGENCY /
we+

PHOTOGRAPHY /
Masayuki Hayashi

Disguise is a flower vase with unique textures created by making multiple layers of wax in a rotary motion. The LED inside lights it up from underneath. Solenoid hits the LED device to generate subtle vibrations. The subtle vibrations create ripples in the water, which are then reacted by the light.

MATERIAL

The spherical vase is made from wax.

MAKING

The wax vase is created by hand, using rotational making method.

CREATIVE

Wax is used as the material. Rather than treating it as part of the process, the wax can be reused simply by melting it, turning it into a versatile, safe, and harmless material for both human and environment.

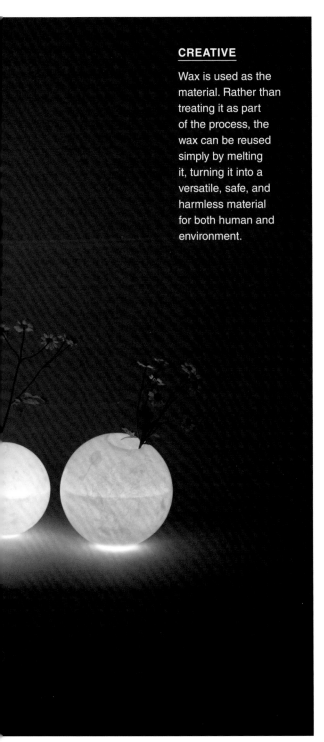

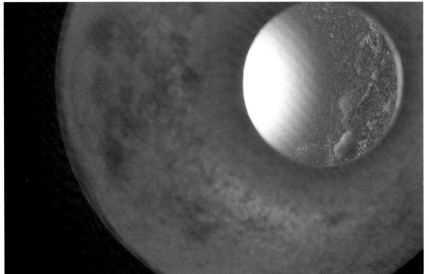

Voltasol

AGENCY /
BAG Disseny Studio

DESIGN /
Xavier Mora, Sandra Compte

CLIENT /
Livingthings

Voltasol is especially designed to move according to the trajectory of the sun, which explains the pot's particular inclination. It is designed to promote the movement of plants and help them grow better. The flowerpot has a semi-conical base that avoids the static nature of conventional pots, thereby creating a slight movement that can either be generated spontaneously or else be induced at will. The simple movement is created on the axis of the pot.

MATERIAL

The pot is handmade with red ceramic from La Bisbal d'Empordà in Spain, with a waterproof treatment. The purity of materials and the respect with which it is manufactured make it a special object—one of those unique and lovable creatures that end up forming a part of the family's emotional landscape.

MAKING

The flowerpot is shaped and created on the wheel by hand.

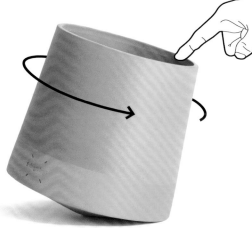

CREATIVE

The plant sway in a breeze. When Voltasol stops again, the sun shines in a new part of the plant and promotes its growth and health. "Voltasol" refers to the formular: sun + plant + movement = voltasol.

V4

AGENCY /
SY DESIGN

DESIGN /
Seung-Yong Song

PHOTOGRAPHY /
Jun-Ho Yum

Lightness and heaviness, lines and lumps, smoothness and roughness, coldness and warmth, V4 presents opposite sensations in one design. All materials and forms balance through the course of colliding and confronting within one volume. The whole series is comprised of vases in four sizes: 160 × 160 × 345/400mm, 205 × 205 × 320/326mm.

CREATIVE

The project is to explore the possibility of the forms, materials, and textures of modern vase.

MATERIAL

The materials used are stainless steel, cement covered chrome paint, and walnut wood.

MAKING

The vase base is created by pouring liquid cement into a certain mold. The vase body is made of wired steel.

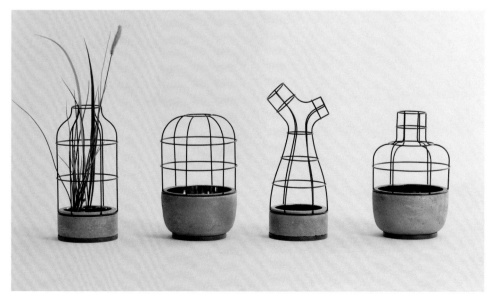

MATERIAL

The tray is made from concrete. The base is made of walnut and oak wood.

MAKING

The tray is created out of concrete making.

Flota Trays

AGENCY /
LaSelva

CLIENT /
Más

PHOTOGRAPHY /
Sergio Bejarano

LaSelva designed a set of concrete trays in collaboration with Iván Zúñiga. The three trays form a game of poka-yoke as each piece fits only with its base. Both the concrete pieces and the wooden pieces are independent to make the transport, packaging, and cleaning easier. Flota is a family of three decorative trays that can work on their own or as a collection of products.

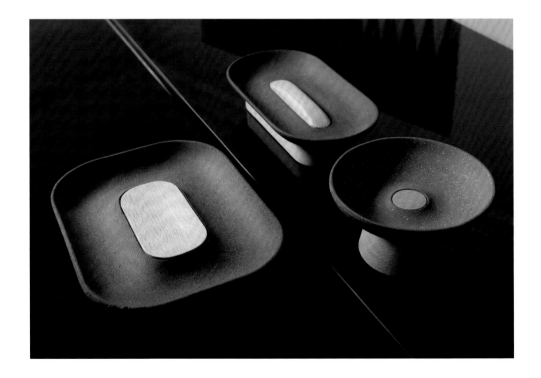

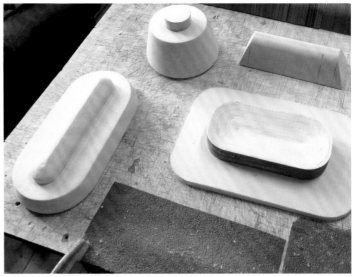

CREATIVE

The project has combined two totally different materials to create rich texture. By lending the game of poka-yoke to the design, the trays become somehow playful.

Purpur

DESIGN /
Roxanne Flick

PHOTOGRAPHY /
Roxanne Flick

An analysis of the cycles in nature show parallels to the cycles of human creation. Both cycles correlate with the viewer's life and are perceived as beautiful. The work intends to show how inspiration through nature is adapted to design. Thus, Roxanne Flick designed a tea set and a table, inspired by the beauty of nature and the beauty of art. Something that is inanimate can become "alive" through the very form that has inspired its creation. The objects reflects the notion of transience, telling a story that correlates with the cycle of the user. The chosen shapes and materials mirror the cycle of the lesser flamingos—their visual appearance, the functions of their body, the choice of their nest site, and their behavior—all are adapted to the design in an abstract way.

CREATIVE

The objects should not only be usable, but speak a language that will fascinate the viewer or the user and triggers one's emotions.

MATERIAL

The work includes a teapot, cups, and sugar/cream jugs made out of porcelain; as well as oak saucers and table made of oak, glass, and granite.

MAKING

The porcelain pieces are manufactured by the technique of slip casting. The saucers and the table are created by woodturning.

Monolith

DESIGN /
Shira Keret

PHOTOGRAPHY /
Hagar Cygler

Water erosion is a process that happens in nature, which can take thousands of years for water to carve its way through rock. The streams intensity and the type of rock will determine the shapes. Shira Keret sped up the process to just a few seconds by carving her Monolith collection of carrera marble homeware with a high-pressure water jet cutting machine. When tweaking the industrial process of water jet cutting, the stream will carve its way to the bottom, not necessarily in a straight line. In such way, it takes a matter of seconds to mimic the natural process and morphology in small scale. Although the technical drawing for the machine are in two-dimensional and extremely basic, the water jet cutting makes the final shapes unpredictable, organic, and one of a kind.

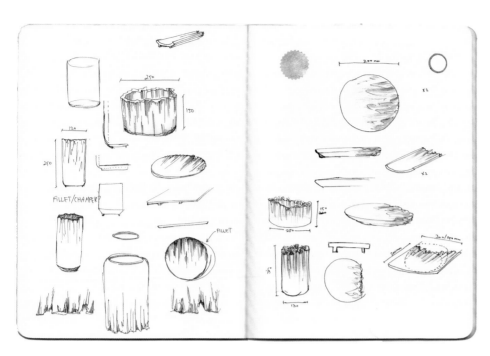

MATERIAL

Carrara marble is the foremost material.

CREATIVE

The streams intensity and the type of rock will determine the shapes, making each piece of work unique and timeless.

MAKING

Waterjet cutting and hand processing were involved. The serving plates and vessels started as basic rectangles and cylinders to be cut on the machine. Shira then began to vary the speed of the machine so the water created jagged edges and patterns across the stone, which were different each time.

Artico

AGENCY /
Sovrappensiero Design Studio

ASSISTANCE /
Fabian Herrera

PHOTOGRAPHY /
Dario De Sirianna

CLIENT /
Incipit Lab

Artico is a pair of ceramic containers with a smooth and organic shape, inspired by a body of water. A little origami-shaped boat and iceberg float stand still on the metallic mirror lid: they resemble reflections on the surface of a calm lake, which seem to have stopped, suspended. The final product looks very simple and natural to let the user to get inspired by the landscape. The project required an intense work of refining and an accurate choice of materials and finishing.

MATERIAL

The product is made from ceramic and mirrored steel.

CREATIVE

With the excellent shape and finishing, the product can serve as containers and decorative objects.

The shape was first created with sketches and computer drawing. It was then finalized on different prototypes before the final product was realized by pouring liquid ceramic into a plaster mold. The lid was realized by a laser-cut.

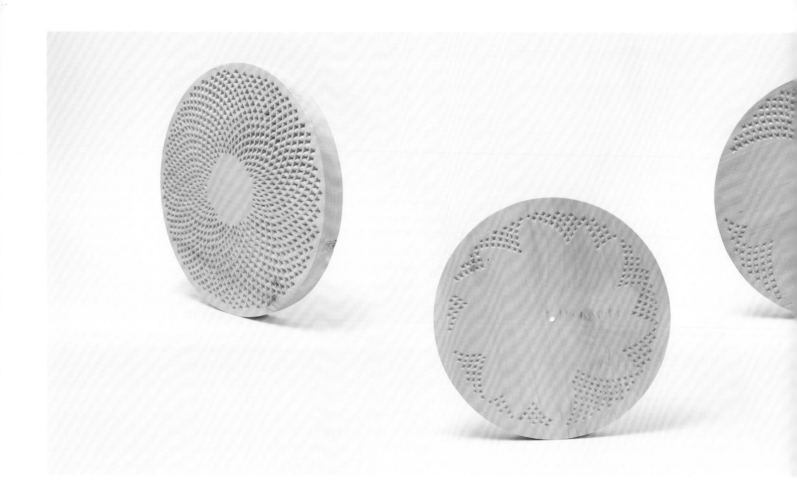

Boards

DESIGN /
Pani Jurek

WOOD CARVING /
Taras Mulyak

PHOTOGRAPHY /
Paweł Heppner, Pani Jurek

The starting point of the design was a reflection on the old rhythm of human work measured by the sun phases. The visual inspiration comes from sunflower, which is considered as a solar plant. The sunflower face filled with seeds resembles Hucul ornaments. Pattern created by nature was transferred by the designer onto the wooden board and "eaten" by a chisel of woodcarver. The craftsman is working on every board, thereby boards with different level of carving are made— every board is unique.

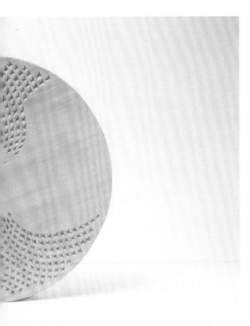

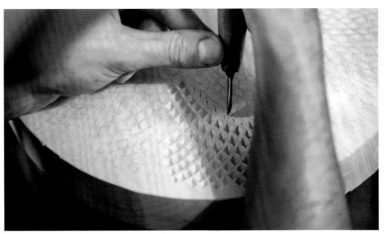

The boards are made of lime wood.

MAKING

The wood are cut into pieces of boards. Patterns on the boards are all carved by hand.

CREATIVE

Multifunctional wood-carved boards can be used as a wall clock shield, a cutting or cheese board, or simply as a decorative piece—the way that the original Hucul plates are used.

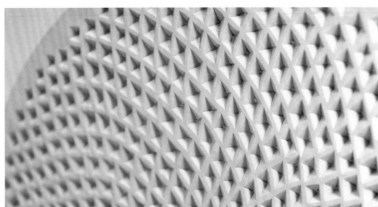

Time Killer

AGENCY /
YUUE

DESIGN /
Weng Xinyu

Time Killer is a tragic clock that attempts to kill itself. If nobody is present, it slowly cuts through its own body. Whenever somebody approaches, it halts. As the blade sinks deeper and deeper with time, the passage of time now becomes a vivid scenario, which leads one to endless contemplation.

MAKING

The prototype started from a section of log found in the woods. It was mill cut to house the mechanical and electronically parts—the heart of the time piece. The development of this essential part was a painful process of trial and error.

MATERIAL

The clock is made of wood, steel, and electronic parts.

CREATIVE

Time Killer is a visual and tangible presentation of the passing of time through a daily object. There is a philosophical thinking beyond the physical form. It is there to remind the user of the cruel fact that time is the invisible force that changes everything, mostly in a destructive way.

KOLO Sand

DESIGN /
Pani Jurek, Piotr Musiałowski

PHOTOGRAPHY /
Paweł Heppner

MATERIAL

Plywood cylinder is covered with an acrylic glass. Inside the cylinder, there is a glass sand. The lighting system is LED.

MAKING

Cylinder and acrylic glass are cut using CNC machine. The other elements are set up by hand.

KOLO Sand comes form a series of cylindrical light objects created by Pani Jurek in collaboration with the architect Piotr Musiałowski. Through tactile play with the object, KOLO Sand allows the users to adjust the light intensity under a touch based on individual needs and moods. KOLO Sand works like an hourglass. After moving mechanism upside down, the sand is slowly covering the light circle with the brightness slowly fading; while the falling sand, accompanied by gentle murmur, creates mesmerizing drawings. Sloping the lamp to the side position can stop the process of falling sand.

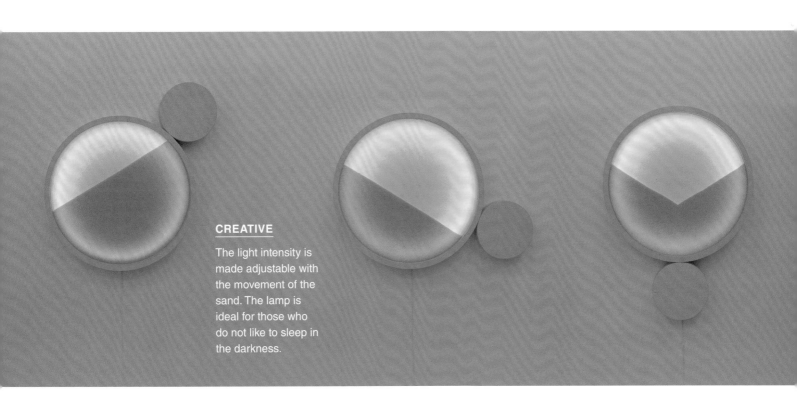

CREATIVE

The light intensity is made adjustable with the movement of the sand. The lamp is ideal for those who do not like to sleep in the darkness.

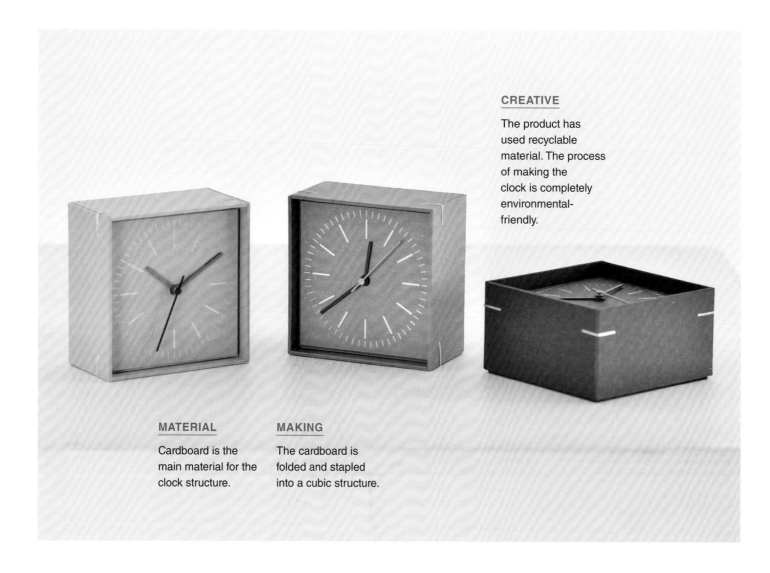

The product has used recyclable material. The process of making the clock is completely environmental-friendly.

MATERIAL

Cardboard is the main material for the clock structure.

MAKING

The cardboard is folded and stapled into a cubic structure.

Box Clock

DESIGN /
Shinya Oguchi

PHOTOGRAPHY /
Shinya Oguchi

Box Clock is a table clock made of two pairs boxes in 2mm thickness. It adopts a traditional technique that holds the edges with staples to form the box.

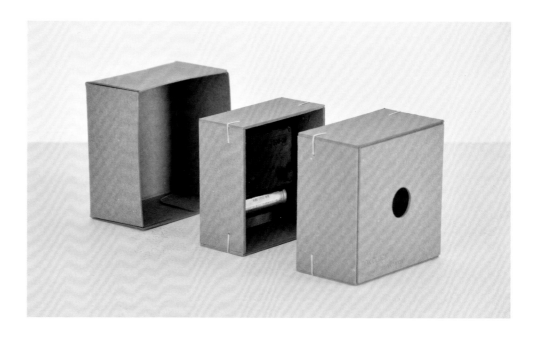

Stryk Match Holder & Striker

CREATIVE

Without manufacturing imprints which would complicate the visual identity of the object, the idea is delivered in a near-pure utility.

MAKING

The product is seamlessly constructed using 3D printing technique.

DESIGN /
Josh Owen

CLIENT /
OTHR

PHOTOGRAPHY /
Elizabeth Lamark

A refinement of the traditional match-stick holder, this multi-faceted heirloom vessel features a striking surface as well as a safe deposit for spent matches. Historic examples of this product have left match disposal to individual choice. Here the life cycle of the match is fully considered. 3D printed technology enables this object to be seamlessly constructed. This allows the undercuts and textures of the object to stay uninterrupted by the constraints of previously employed fabrication or mold-making techniques.

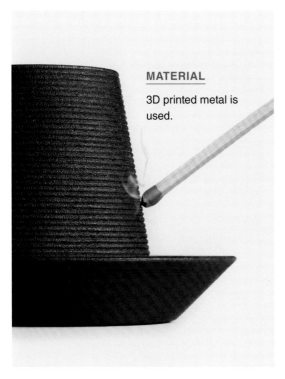

MATERIAL

3D printed metal is used.

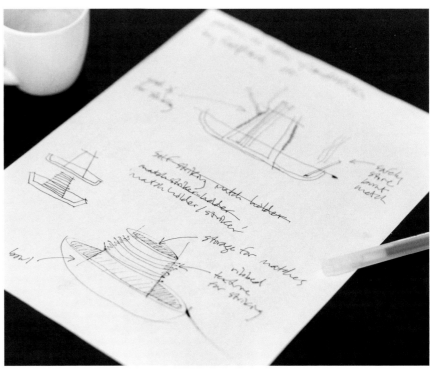

Sunset

AGENCY /
nendo

PHOTOGRAPHY /
Akihiro Yoshida

Nendo created Sunset for its byIn homeware range. It appears to be a normal white candle. But once lit, the centre of the candle begins to change colors as it burns: first to yellow, then orange, red, purple, and finally to blue. These colors reflect faintly off of the white wax surrounding the flame.

The transition of colors is inspired by the shifting shades of light that paint the sunset sky. Each color has its own accompanying scent: bergamot, lemongrass, sweet marjoram, lavender, and geranium.

MATERIAL

The candles are made of wax with various aromas added.

CREATIVE

Not only does the candle provide illumination, but the transition of colors also serves as a reminder of the passage of time.

MAKING

The process involves making the wick, preparing the wax base, adding desired perfumes, making the candles, and consolidating the wax around the wick using extrusion machines.

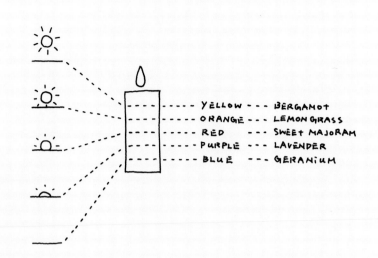

YELLOW --- BERGAMOT
ORANGE --- LEMON GRASS
RED --- SWEET MAJORAM
PURPLE --- LAVENDER
BLUE --- GERANIUM

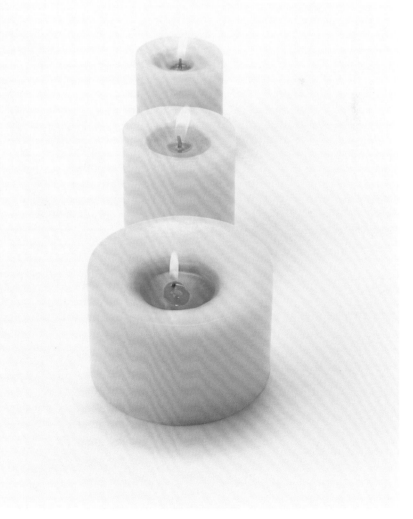

Octagono Candlestick

DESIGN /
Katia Tolstykh

Octagono candlestick is a functional design that can carry one to three candles and double as a vase. By turning the Octagono copper elements, things will change—settings, stories, and even the way that one interprets things. With this project, one can combine flowers, candles, leaves, limbs—whatever he or she wants, to create his or her own story and mood.

MATERIAL

Copper and marble are used for this project.

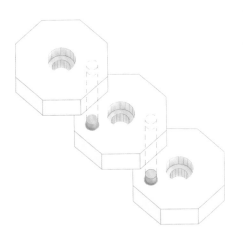

MAKING

The marble are cut by machine. The copper are jointed and made movable.

CREATIVE

The project gives the user a chance to decide how the product functions.

Candela
Candle Holders

AGENCY /
LaSelva

CLIENT /
Más

PHOTOGRAPHY /
Sergio Bejarano

Candela is inspired directly by the work of the architect Félix Candela for its forms and materiality. The candle holder takes advantage of the properties of concrete to achieve a product that is easy to produce and to expand into a family. Candela works as an individual piece and as a set. The candle continues the shape of the base to obtain an integrated and logic object.

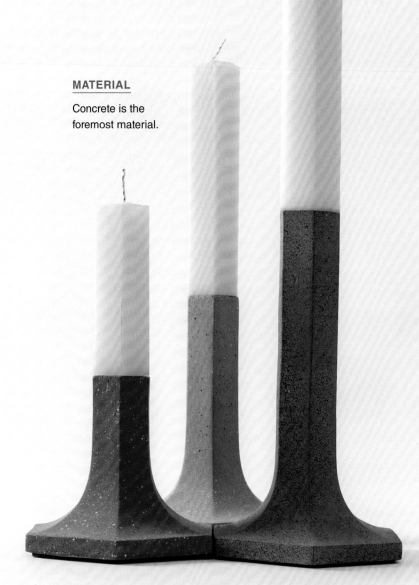

MATERIAL

Concrete is the foremost material.

CREATIVE

Modularity is the base of Candela.

MAKING

The holder base is made by pouring liquid concrete into the mould.

NOSE

DESIGN /
Quentin de Coster

PHOTOGRAPHY /
Stéphanie Derouaux

Nose is a minimal candle holder resembling an abstract creature whose nose serves to hold the candle. The object is made of two laser cut and welded steel pieces. With or without candle, Nose is a sculptural candle holder that adds a touch of poetry to the user's interior.

MATERIAL

Powder coated steel is used to create this project.

MAKING

The steel is laser-cut and welded.

CREATIVE

This candle holder is like a piece of art. It is an object that makes sense even when people do not use it.

Meji

AGENCY /
nendo

PHOTOGRAPHY /
Akihiro Yoshida

Typical umbrella stand looks like either a huge container or a box full of holes and cannot help but seem out of place when not holding any umbrellas. By using grooves instead of holes, this umbrella stand maintains a simple, clean appearance. The design's motif takes inspiration from the joints of a tiled floor. When an umbrella is set into the grooves, the product becomes an umbrella stand. It does not look out of place when not in use, and maintains a neat appearance even when multiple stands are lined up in an entryway. Users press the spike of their umbrella into the centre until it is held vertically in place. Nendo created the objects for its byIn homeware range. Options include a single-umbrella stand and a three-umbrella stand, each available in five colors, including black, white and a light purple-grey shade.

MATERIAL

The stand is made using a dense resin known as Polystone. This is then covered with silicone, which offers excellent pliability and durability.

MAKING

The Meji umbrella stand is a silicone-covered resin block with a cross shape cut into its top.

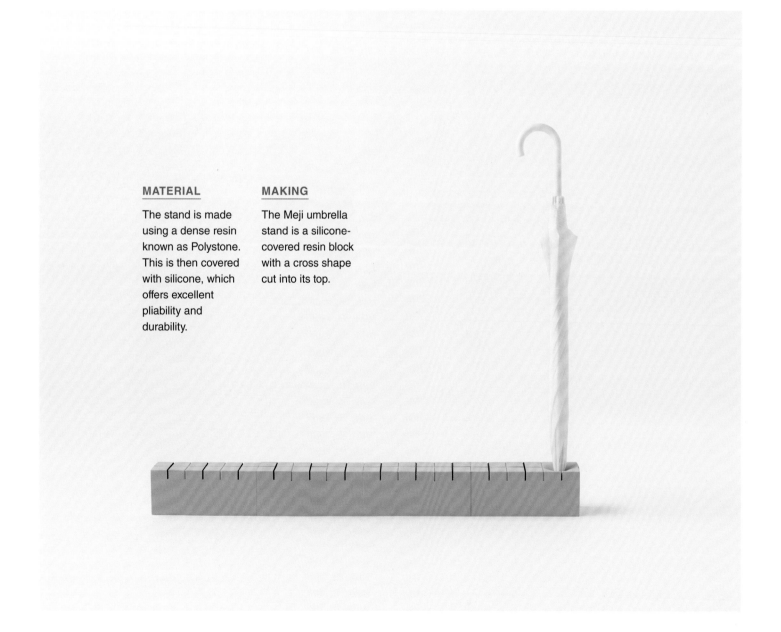

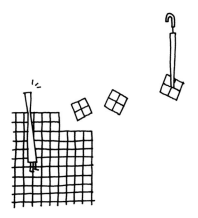

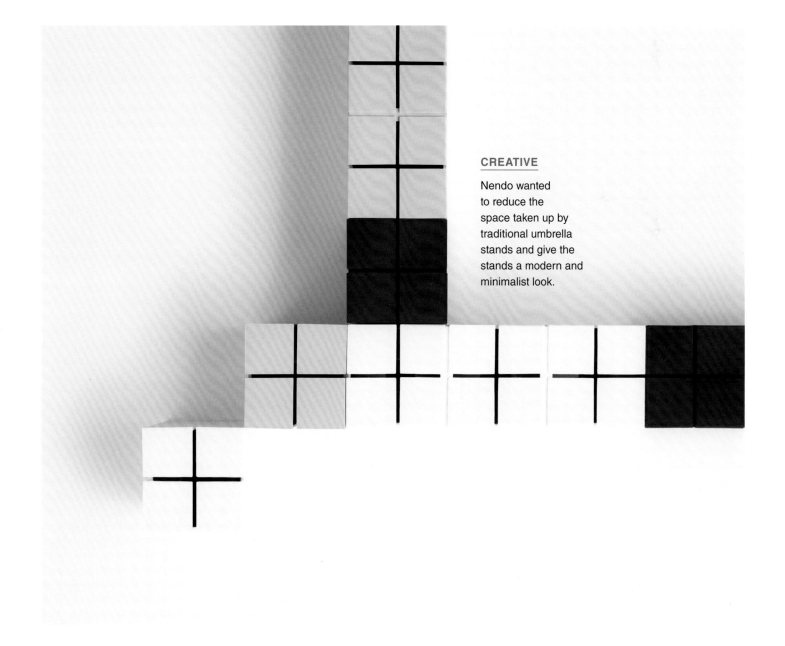

CREATIVE

Nendo wanted to reduce the space taken up by traditional umbrella stands and give the stands a modern and minimalist look.

Cuecos

AGENCY /
Designo Patagonia

DESIGN /
Kaleb Cárdenas

ART DIRECTION /
Manu Rapoport, Martín Sabatini

Cuecos is a collection of containers reflecting the transformation of matter through time. This unusual set consists of spice containers for contemporary kitchens as well as storage items for personal belongings. The project is a collaboration between Argentinian studio Designo Patagonia and Kaleb Cárdenas. Kaleb has created the project during his six-month internship in the studio.

MATERIAL

Keen in mixing industrial technology with high-qualified craft, Kaleb creates

Cuecos series with local materials. Lenga wood and endemic rocks are used to make this project.

CREATIVE

The studio, alongside the industrial designer, has completed a sustainable framework by using local material and encouraging the use of recyclable goods.

MAKING

They process and cut lenga wood into desirable shape with machine, and polish it with olive oil and turpentine finish. Endemic pebbles are carefully selected and used, which go well with the wood texture.

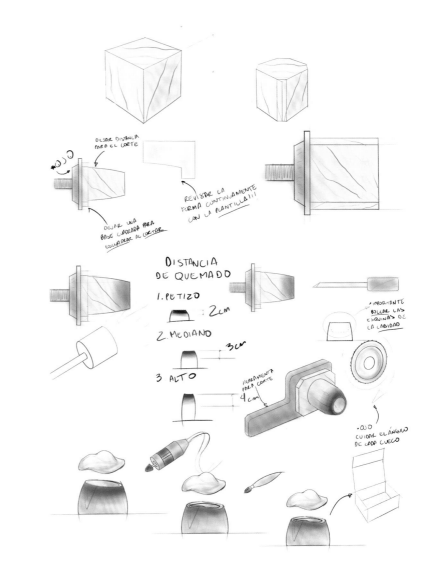

Katerina

DESIGN /
Yaroslav Misonzhnikov

PHOTOGRAPHY /
Mitya Ganopolsky, Vasily Bulanov

Katerina is a collection of folding fan made with Vologda laces (a kind of Russian folk art), mirror, and a comb. Lace pattern was based on an existing traditional element and combined with a minimalistic fan shape. By using thread of different thicknesses the gradient effect was achieved. The designer dedicated this collection to his grandmother, Katerina, who lived in Vologda and used to tell him stories about her mother making lace in a izba—a traditional Russian timber wooden chalet.

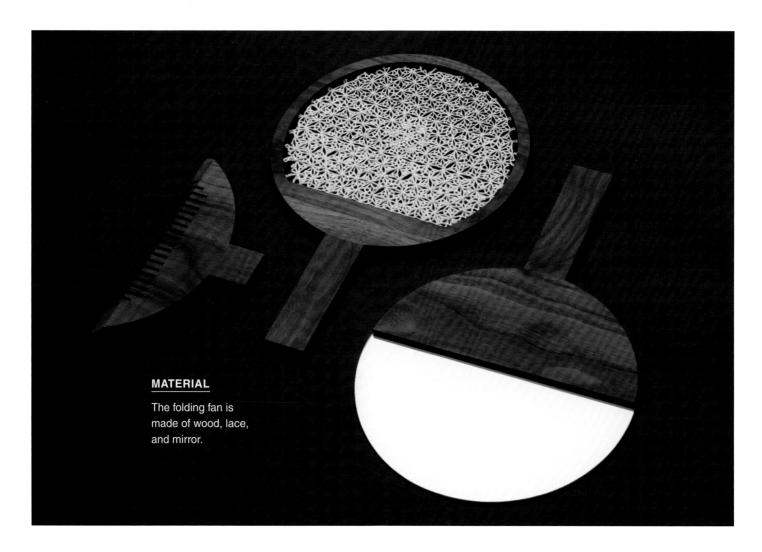

MATERIAL

The folding fan is made of wood, lace, and mirror.

MAKING

Lace pattern is based on traditional design and achieved by using thread of different thicknesses. This intricate and complex geometry of the handmade lace was then paired with a natural timber in rich tones and grain.

CREATIVE

This project was to revive or "incarnate" these traditional Russian folk arts and crafts, by reinterpreting them within a contemporary context.

Suie

DESIGN /
**Nolwenn Michea, Donia Ouertani,
Flora Koel**

CLIENT /
**International Design Biennale of Saint-
Etienne, France 2017**

PHOTOGRAPHY /
**Nolwenn Michea, Donia Ouertani,
Flora Koel**

Suie is a collection of three small objects to be disseminated at home—a paperweight, a diffuser of essential oils, and a card holder. In its conical shape and coal-like texture, Suie reminds the users of the crassiers (hills of coal) of Saint-Etienne and embodies the theme of the International Design Biennale. With the simple form, these objects seem enigmatic.

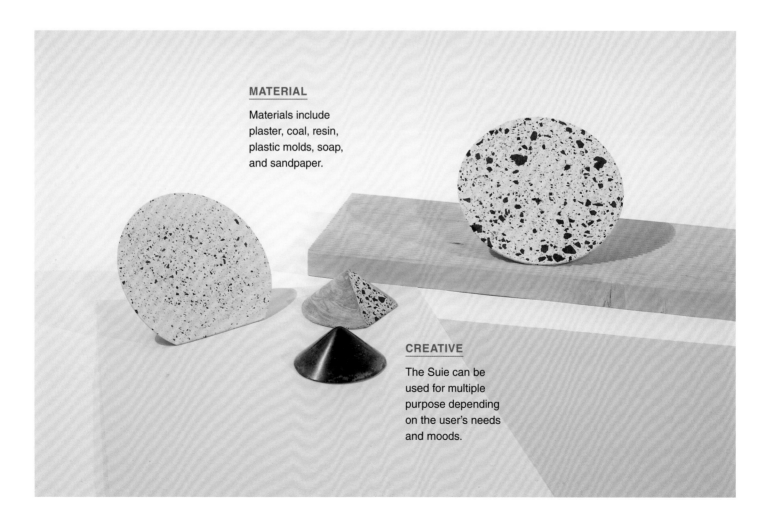

MATERIAL

Materials include plaster, coal, resin, plastic molds, soap, and sandpaper.

CREATIVE

The Suie can be used for multiple purpose depending on the user's needs and moods.

MAKING

The designers worked as a team. They made different samples of plaster and coal to get the color and the texture wanted. They also made thermoformed plastic molds in which the mixture was poured. It took about a day to dry the molded piece.

Ovo

AGENCY /
Monitillo Marmi
DESIGN /
May Day Design, Andrea Maldifassi

Ovo is an amplifier for iPhone 5, 6 and 7 in white carrara marble, which works without electricity. It is the shape of the object that amplifies the sound. Uniting the Apulian tradition of stone craftsmanship with cutting-edge product manufacturing, Monitillo Marmi has collaborated with May Day Design to realize "Ovo," a passive iphone amplifier made from carrara marble. The essence of the raw material is highly considered and maintained while revealing its properties with a contemporary quality.

The Ovo model is equipped with a milled slot to hold either an iphone 5 or 6, while its internal core follows mathematical formulas to maximize the most efficient amplification of the sound, despite its small size. Its shape has been painstakingly perfected in order to obtain a smooth, cylindrical composition with two base points, allowing the object to be inclined in different directions with distinct sources for the acoustic flow to traverse.

MATERIAL

White carrara marble is the foremost material.

MAKING

The amplifier's shape is obtained through the slow and accurate removal of marble from a full carrara slab; these mammoth pieces are carefully selected to avoid cracks and impurities, processed with CNC technology and finally hand-finished in order to achieve a smooth outer surface and a slightly grooved inner texture.

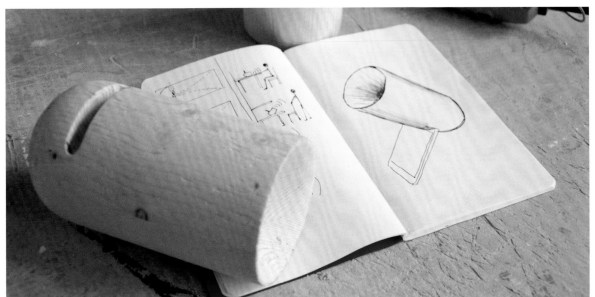

CREATIVE

Ovo expresses the binomials of technology and tradition, digital and analog, artisanship and innovation.

Faber-Modern Stoneware

AGENCY /
Oddly Studio

DESIGN /
Youngmin Kang

PHOTOGRAPHY /
Youngmin Kang

People have lots of tools in daily life and normally use them for intended purposes; while sometimes, however, exception occurs. For example, people may use a computer mouse for holding a paper, though this may not be the original purpose of which the mouse is designed. People are familiar with the mouse's shape and weight and know that it fits well when holding paper pieces. Youngmin Kang has faced similar situation in daily life. Such experiences inspire him to wonder where current tool shapes come into being and how people can use tools instinctually depending on their shapes. To find the answer, he created "Faber," tracing back to primitive ages where human being started to use raw materials or natural objects for the first time.

MATERIAL

To give a modern impression to the product, Kang chose brass. He wanted to make a definite difference with stone of the Paleolithic age.

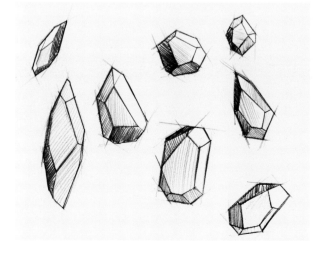

MAKING

The designers focused on a tool called "stone." In order to obtain the form of stoneware, the designers made rocks with gypsum and wiped them directly to get appropriate forms. Based on the rocks, they designed a polygonal stoneware using a 3D printer. After that, they obtained brass products by making gypsum molds with the 3D prints.

CREATIVE

The functions of the product are not determined. It acts as a suitable material for a modern desk as well as a decorative element. People can use the product depending on their shapes, just like what the ancestors did.

Brass Object Cat

DESIGN /
Jaejin Lee

PHOTOGRAPHY /
Jaejin Lee

Curiosity of a cat can be known by their actions and postures. Brass Object Cat is done by observing postures of cats in ordinary life and making it into three-dimensional structures.

The final product is made of brass. It can be served as paper weight, storage for jewelry such as rings, or simply a decorative piece on desk.

ANIMOLIC
BRASS OBJECT
C02

PRODUCT NO. AMC02 weight. 86g
Designed by soosu, manufactured by daight

MATERIAL

Brass is the main material of the product.

CREATIVE

The product perfectly mirrors the postures and characteristics of cats.

MAKING

The process involves sketching, 3D modeling, 3D printing, making mold, making wax, brass casting, sanding the structure, and finishing.

"Poyekhali!" Desktop Organizer

AGENCY /
52 FACTORY

"Poyekhali!" is dedicated to the first outstanding achievements in space exploration. "Poyekhali" means "Off we go" in Russian, which is a famous phrase said by the first cosmonaut Yuri Gagarin during the first manned space ship VOSTOK-1 launch in 1961. The phrase became a symbol of human evolution in space era. "Poyekhali!" includes the following items: VOSTOK-1 writing utensils holder, with the space ship served as a prototype; LUNOKHOD-1 stationery/jewelry box inspired by the shape of the remote-controlled self-propelled Lunokhod (lunar rover) that successfully completed its mission on the Moon's surface; MOON, a multifunctional platform, designed to resemble the lunar surface, with basic lunar elements such as Sea of Serenity for pins/needles, Copernicus Crater for clips, Sea of Showers and Ocean of Storms for erasers and small paraphernalia, and Tycho Crater for tape/hair bands.

MATERIAL

The series is made of wood and steel.

MAKING

The wood is delicately cut into desired shape.

CREATIVE

It celebrates the human's advance in space exploration using modern design language.

Roro

DESIGN /
Ken Chen

ART DIRECTION /
Tom Weis

Toys are playful, fanciful, and timeless; ceramic tableware sets are delicate, functional, and fragile. Roro is an enjoyable toy car, and a useful tableware for the young and young-at-heart users who would use it for joy and treat it with care.

MATERIAL

The body of the car is made of ceramic. The wheel and the plug is made of wood.

MAKING

Slip casting is required to make the ceramic car body.

CREATIVE

The project has combined both functionality and playfulness.

Tropical Bird

AGENCY /
SWNA

DESIGN /
Sukwoo Lee, Jueun Choi

Tropical bird can carry pen and pencil on the top. The wooden birds are each made with maple wood. The users can feel the natural texture of the wood. Pens and pencils being placed on the top of Tropical bird are like feathers. With different colors of the pens, the users can imagine the pen container as any type of bird.

MATERIAL

Maple wood is the main material.

MAKING

The wood is processed by wood CNC machine.

CREATIVE

Tropical bird is a design combining functionality and beauty. Tropical bird perched on the desk will make the user feel bright and breezy.

MATERIAL

The main material is solid oak, discarded residues collected from carpentry product.

Russian Avant-Garde Desktop Organizer

AGENCY /
52 FACTORY

Russian design agency 52 Factory has created a series of wooden desktop organizer, dedicated to the Russian avant-garde architectures. The set is inspired by the remarkable period in Russian architecture. The set consists of 10 wooden elements, each having a function of its own, ranging from pencil sharpener to ruler, docking station for smart phone, holders for business cards, post-it notes and erasers, paper clips magnet holder, adhesive tape dispenser, and organizer for pens.

Each piece of the design corresponds accordingly to a landmark of the Russian avant-garde structure—Communication Industry Workers' Palace of Culture, Chimney of the Red Banner Textile Factory, Communal House of the Textile Institute, Bakhmetevsky Bus Garage, Moscow Raysoviet (District Council), the Melnikov House, Round Bath-House. Comprised of a few small functional items, the desktop organizer set is 52 Factory's tribute to all lovers of Russian avant-garde.

MAKING

The wood is delicately cut into desired shape.

CREATIVE

The designers aspire to create a really functional object, taking into account one of the basic rules of constructivism—the rational justification of elements, rather than a thing for nonfunctional beauty.

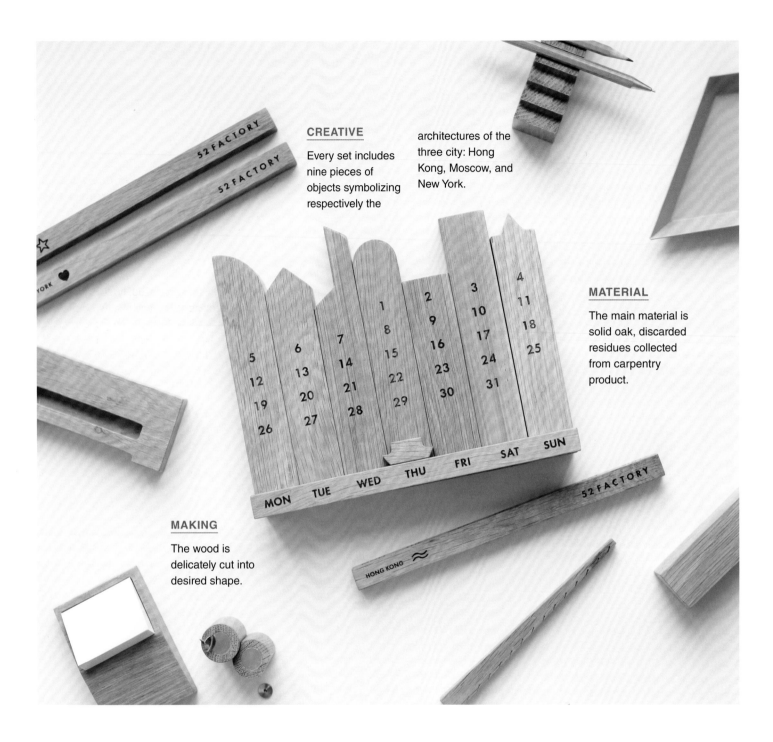

CREATIVE

Every set includes nine pieces of objects symbolizing respectively the architectures of the three city: Hong Kong, Moscow, and New York.

MATERIAL

The main material is solid oak, discarded residues collected from carpentry product.

MAKING

The wood is delicately cut into desired shape.

Wooden Metropolises Eternal Calendars

AGENCY /
52 FACTORY

Russian agency 52 Factory has presented a series of three eternal calendars dedicated to the metropolises of Hong Kong, Moscow, and New York. Each element of the set corresponds to an existing building of the given city, with the most symbolic or indigenous metropolis' vehicle used to mark the current day of the week, such as Hong Kong boat, "Moskvich" car, and New York taxi respectively. By rotating the facets of the buildings to correspond to the current month's view, any of the possible combinations can be obtained. The size of calendar is 21 × 4 × 17cm.

Echid

DESIGN /
Jaejin Lee

PHOTOGRAPHY /
Jaejin Lee

Jaejin Lee has drawn inspiration from a plant called Echinops. Echinops is a genus of about 120 species of flowering plants in the family Asteraceae, commonly known as globe thistles. They have spiny foliage and produce blue or white spherical flower heads. Every time when Jaejin looks at Echinops's head, he felt like he was looking at the face of a mischievous baby. So he named the product "Echid," a compound composed of "Echinops" and "child." The product can be a toy or decorative object, which is a lot of fun.

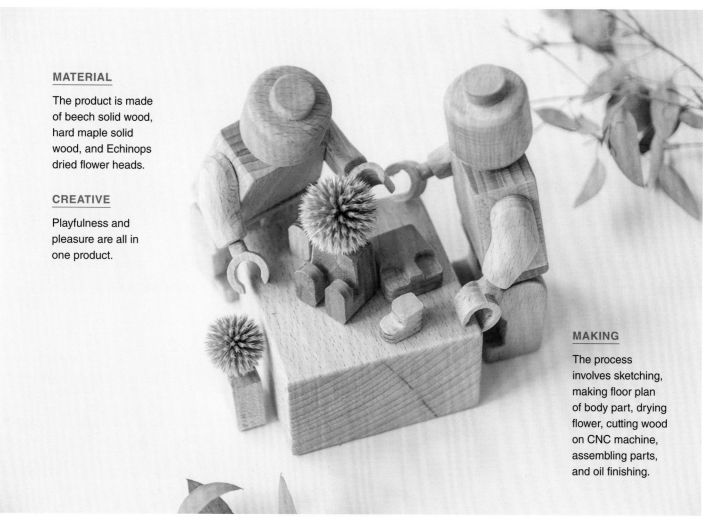

MATERIAL

The product is made of beech solid wood, hard maple solid wood, and Echinops dried flower heads.

CREATIVE

Playfulness and pleasure are all in one product.

MAKING

The process involves sketching, making floor plan of body part, drying flower, cutting wood on CNC machine, assembling parts, and oil finishing.

Perpetuum Calendar

AGENCY /
Yonoh

CLIENT /
OTHR

Inspired by the architecture of the industrial boom, Perpetuum's shape is a nod to the "sawtooth" roofs of factories built in the 1920s and 1930s. The calendar's 3D printed fabric base emulates the era's move towards the synthetic, gracefully guiding an antiquated material into the 21st century.

MATERIAL

The base is 3D printed in fabric-like plastic, with 14K gold-plated timepieces.

MAKING

Three-dimensional printed making is required.

CREATIVE

It pays tribute to modern industrial design and knocks open the applications of new material in design.

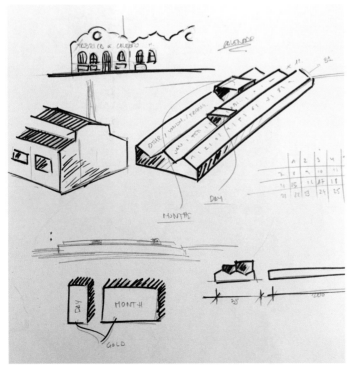

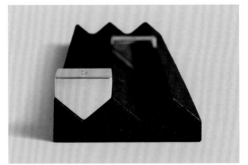

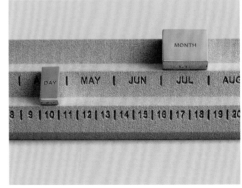

INDEX

52 FACTORY

52 FACTORY is established in 2014 by Nasya Kopteva and Sasha Braulov from St. Petersburg, with a mission of inventing and creating special items for conscious and harmonious life. 52 FACTORY is one of the participants of SaloneSatellite WorldWide Moscow and winners/nominees of several international awards, including Design and Design International Awards, German Design Awards and ADD Awards.
52factory.ru
p222-223, p228-229, p230

alien and monkey

Alien and monkey is a Barcelona based studio founded by Marc Nicolau and Daishu Ma. They currently work on small objects, refining the process and exploring further applications for the material, sand.
alienandmonkey.com
p044-045, p140-141

Anastasiya Koshcheeva

Anastasiya Koshcheeva was born and raised in Krasnoyarsk, Siberia. In 2006 she made Germany her second home, commuting between Berlin, Moscow and Krasnoyarsk. She explores material's unique potential, aesthetic features, and haptic qualities in an experimental way. Her work is characterized by the combination of contrasting textures, colors, and skills.
www.anastasiyakoshcheeva.com
p047, p052-053, p126-127

Ankit Tatiya

Ankit Tatiya's never-ending curiosity shapes her as a person and a designer. Design allows her to interact with creative people and experience a very fast paced life. Design gives her a unique perspective on life and a chance to express such view through her work.
www.behance.net/ankittatiya1234
P148

Anna Gudmundsdottir

Anna Gudmundsdottir is a Swedish/Icelandic industrial designer based in Malmö, Sweden. She recently graduated from the School of Industrial Design at Lund University in Sweden and is currently working from her own studio. Her work mainly revolves around sustainability in consumption and production.
www.annagudmundsdottir.com
p176-179

BAG Disseny Studio

BAG Disseny Studio is a creative corporation founded by Sandra Compte and Xavier Mora in 2002. As a multidisciplinary studio with offices in Barcelona, Andorra, and Girona, the studio dedicates to create new codes and search for new visual forms of communication. Simple and direct solutions are how they define themselves.
www.bagdisseny.com
p184-185

Carl Kleiner

Carl Kleiner is mostly known for still-life photography. Together with his wife and a colleague, they form a studio in Stockholm that focuses on images. The Posture vases are the first product designs to be launched from the studio.
www.carlkleiner.com
p180-181

Carlo Contin

Carlo Contin opened his design and interior architecture firm in 1998, after several years of working as an entrepreneur in his family's company specialized in tailor-made furniture. He made his debut as a designer by presenting his first works at the Salone Satellite in 1999.

Ever since then he has been collaborating with some of the most famous design companies in Italian and International scenario, besides participating in a number of exhibitions both at home and abroad.
www.carlocontin.it
p076-077, p086-089

Chen Min Office

Chen Min Office is a multi-faceted design practice established by Chen Min whose production ranges from product to interior architecture. Born in 1980 in China, Chen was trained at Köln International School of Design in Germany. He has completed his Bachelor of Design at the Design Academy Eindhoven and MA degree at Domus Academy in Milan. In 2010 he came back to China and has been invited to give lecture at some academies including China Central Academy of Fine Arts and Tsinghua University. He has developed a worldwide reputation for several award-winning design projects.
www.chen-min.com
p016-017

Dackelid-Form

Dackelid-Form is founded by Nathalie Dackelid, a young daydreamer and furniture designer living in Stockholm, Sweden. She strives for designs that are true to the materials and unveil the properties of the materials in a visually and sustainable manner.
www.dackelid-form.portfoliobox.se
p022-023

Daphna Laurens

Daphna Laurens is the unification of Daphna Isaacs Burggraaf and Laurens Manders established in 2008. Daphna Laurens aspires to find a combination between industrial design, applied art, and fine art. They give shape to an idea, object, product or concept. They create characteristic products and objects with sophisticated combinations of shapes, materials, and colors.
www.daphnalaurens.nl
p096-097, p122-123

Design Studio PESI

Design Studio PESI is a Seoul-based studio. They find new possibility by reinterpreting an object from their point of view without losing its essentials.
www.designstudiopesi.com
P080-081

Dragos Motica Studio

Founded in 2008, Dragos Motica Studio is a multidisciplinary studio based in Bucharest. Working within the fields of architecture, interior design, product design, and graphic design, the studio combines projects ranging from experimental works in limited editions to serial products. The studio was awarded A' Design Award Gold Medal for "/" Lamp. The studio's projects have been featured in many publications worldwide, both online and in print.
www.dragosmotica.ro
p012-013, p124-125, p132-133

Elena Rogna

Elena Rogna is a young, bubbly Italian designer. Taking inspiration from reality, she likes to follow and answer both real needs and real emotions. By "real," it refers to her love of reading everyday life and transforming it with her design. Though she is an industrial designer, she enjoys mixing art and design, unique pieces and industrial objects.
www.elenarogna.it
p050-051

Fernando Laposse

Born in Paris, Fernando Laposse is a London based Mexican designer. He has obtained a BA in Product Design at Central Saint Martins in 2012. His work is deeply rooted in material experimentation and craft with a great emphasis on self production and DIY culture.

Fernando strives to transform materials that are cheap or readily available, so as to make crossovers between product design and gastronomy.
www.fernandolaposse.com
p162

Fritsch-Durisotti

Fritsch-Durisotti is a creation studio led by curiosity. Always seeking new challenges, the studio systematically places use and users at the centre of its design. Beyond the services that the studio carries out for its clients, it keeps a space of freedom. Fritsch-Durisotti in fact contributes its "free expressions" to the societal transformations by sharing its positive vision of the future.
www.fritsch-durisotti.com
p058-059, p060-061, p110-111

Gerardo Osio

Gerardo Osio is a product design brand founded in 2013 by Gerardo Sandoval Osio, a mexican product designer graduated at Universidad Autónoma de Nuevo León. The studio focuses on offering product design related services. Gerardo Osio's work has gained a place in many exhibitions, including Generación DECODE 2014 and 2015, Tokyo Design Week 2016, and Milan Design Week 2017.
www.gerardoosio.com
p166-167

Hanna Bramford

Hanna Bramford originated from Gotland, Sweden. She is currently studying Architect at Lund School of Architecture.
www.hannabramford.se
p028-029

HATTERN

Hattern, a design studio based in Seoul, South Korea, focuses on up-cycling and extracting patterns from waste and different combinations of materials.

They strive to design practical and beautiful everyday items.
www.hattern.com
p014-015

Hiperobjetos

Hiperobjetos is created by Mexican designers Herminio Menchaca and Eduardo Hernández for the experience and research on technical and craft workshops in Japan with the support of some organizations: Japanese International Cooperation Agency, National Council of Science and Technology from Mexico and Kyoto Institute of Technology. They believe that innovation is part of the new evolution of crafts and they describe it as "hyper objects," a greater value added to an object.
www.hiperobjetos.com
p084-085

ilsangisang

Ilsangisang always observes daily life in which people, nature, and objects are mingled with each other. Through their own design language—delicate wit—they create living and interior design products that are both beautiful and useful.
www.ilsangisang.com
p134-137

Iratzoki Lizaso

Iratzoki Lizaso is an industrial design studio established by Jean Louis Iratzoki and Ander Lizaso in the Basque Country in 2016. Ably supported by their experienced team, they work closely with both small companies and large corporations.

Their work encompasses various areas of design: home and office furniture, textiles, lighting, ephemeral architecture, and accessories.
www.iratzoki-lizaso.com
p152-153

Jaejin Lee

Jaejin Lee is a designer based in Seoul, Korea. He raises cats and draws inspiration from them to create illustrations and 3D graphic works, and then turn them into visible craftwork.
www.imajine.tv
p104-105, p120-121, p220-221, p231

Jiyoun Kim

Jiyoun Kim graduated from Hongik University in 2009 and became the manager of the North American branch of Pantech Mobile Device Design. During his stay in Pantech, he started his own company, JiyounKim Studio, and worked on projects for sound systems, medical machines, and other important devices. In 2014, he received his EMBA at Sung-Kyun-Kwan University. Then he moved to HSAD and created advertisements for LG. Later he founded Over the Rainbow, offering design projects and services for brand consultations. Currently he works as a brand consultant for various companies and has won the Reddot and IF awards.
www.jiyounkim.com
p042-043

Jongha Choi

Jongha Choi originates from South Korea. He has gained a BA and MFA degree in Sculpture at Seoul National University in 2008. In 2015 he has obtained a MA degree in Contextual Design at the Design Academy Eindhoven in the Netherlands.
www.jonghachoi.com
p036-037

Josh Owen

Josh Owen is a designer and professor of Industrial Design at Rochester Institute of Technology in Rochester, New York. His work has been featured at the Venice Biennale and is in the permanent design collections of the Centre Georges Pompidou, Chicago Athenaeum, Musée des Beaux-Arts de Montreal, National Museum of American Jewish History, Philadelphia Museum of Art, and the Taiwan Design Museum, among others. His home/design, furniture, and office products are regularly featured in design books, periodicals, and in critical design discourse.
www.joshowen.com
p201

Juan Cappa

Copenhagen-based designer Juan Cappa designs and makes furniture and lightning objects with the intention of showing the potential of different crafts and techniques in contemporary design. His design is based on the work and experimentation with natural materials and traditional crafts from around the world.
www.juancappa.com
p046, p102-103

Julius Graupner

Julius Graupner is an industrial designer currently living in Munich. Since he worked on his Bachelor degree in 2008, he had been working on projects of different scales in different fields. His clients range from major companies like Airbus, BMW, Linde to startups like design offices or creative hobbyists.
www.juliusgraupner.com
p161

Juno Jeon

Juno Jeon is a Korean-born furniture designer based in the Netherlands. He brings seemingly ordinary objects to life with his unique designs. His work centers on interactions between objects and people. He has received the New Talent award at the DMY International Design Festival in 2016.
www.junojunos.com
p026-027, p098-101

KAIRI EGUCHI DESIGN

Established in 2008 by Kairi Eguchi, KED is a Japanese industrial design studio based in Osaka. With the studio's philosophy "discover the unknowns," KED not only provides standard design service, but also continues expanding its services such as product planning, design strategy, etc., so as to provide elegant and new approachs for a better user experience. With the exhibition experience at Milan's Salone Satellite for three times, KED has signaled the start of numerous overseas exhibitions and projects/collaborations throughout the international design arena.
kairi-eguchi.com
p094-095, p108-109, p154-155

Kaleb Cárdenas

Kaleb Cárdenas has obtained a Bachelor degree in Industrial Design at Tecnologico de Monterrey, in Guadalajara, Mexico. Kaleb is seeking to incorporate several design disciplines to his work in a holistic and human centered way to solve everyday problems with multidisciplinary teams.
www.kalebcardenas.mx
p020-021, p210-211

Katia Tolstykh

Katia Tolstykh is a Berlin based multi-disciplinary designer from Saint-Petersburg, Russia. She works on interior, furniture, and product design. She is also the co-owner of SUPAFORM STUDIO.
www.katiatolstykh.com
p204-205

Ken Chen

Ken Chen was born and raised in Shenzhen, China. He is currently a graduating senior at Rhode Island School of Design majored in Industrial Design. As a designer and maker, he is passionate about creating unique objects with functionality by experimenting simple form, tactility, and materials.
ken-chen.com
p070-071, p144-145, p160, p224-225

Knots Studio

Knots Studio was established in 2013 by Neta Tesler, a graduate in the Textile Department at the Shenkar College of Engineering and Design. In her senior year, Neta was inspired by the aesthetics of the nautical world. She researched and experimented with different materials and found a special tying technique, with which she used to design her first line of products. After graduation, Neta continued developing her studio, which now sells home décor products to various distributors around the world.

www.knots-studio.com
p106

LaSelva

LaSelva is a design studio operating from Spain and Mexico, founded by Manuel Bañó and David Galvañ. After years of experience working with international brands such as BoConcept, UCH CEU University, John Lewis, University of Valencia, they cover ranges of products based on new needs and user profiles, with a great fixation for detail and the study of new materials.

www.laselvastudio.es
p188-189, p206

Line Design Studio

Line Design Studio is a young team dedicated to architecture and design established by Mikhail Lenko and Alexander Vezlomtsev in 2015. The main idea that guides the team is to create an aesthetic product that is simple and understandable to the user.

www.ldinterior.com
p018-019

Lisa Ertel

Lisa Ertel was born in 1990. She is currently a student at the Karlsruhe University of Arts and Design in Germany.

www.lisaertel.com
p024-025

Maison Deux

Maison Deux is a home and living brand for kids and their parents. It is founded to design fun, minimalist products for contemporary homes. All their products are crafted from high-quality and natural materials that last for generations. They aim for simple and iconic products with a playful twist.

www.maisondeux.com
p030-031

Malika Novi

Malika Novi is a product and interior designer, 3D render specialist based in Italy. She likes fashion, graphic, photography, and art.

www.malikanovi.com
p138-139

Mario Tsai Studio

Mario Tsai Studio, established by Mario Tsai, focuses on furniture design and product design. Mario always insists on a moderation concept: use less, design better; and he names it "soft minimalism." He looks for a way to interact with people through design, and explore the materials that improve the society and environment.

www.mariotsai.studio
p082-083

Martín Azúa

Martín Azúa is a Basque designer working in Barcelona since 1994. Graduated in Fine Arts from the University of Barcelona, he considers experimental methods as a fundamental part of the design process. Since 2007, his "Basic House" project has been part of the permanent collection of MOMA in New York. He also has pieces in the collection of the Barcelona Design Museum and in different public or private collections. He has won some famous design awards, including Design Plus, AD Award.

www.martinazua.com
p130-131, p168-169

Moisés Hernández

Moisés Hernández is a Mexican born designer based in Mexico City. His hometown, as well as Mexican objects, traditions, textures, social contrast, and chromatic diversity are elements that influence his work. Moisés graduated with a Master degree in Product Design at ECAL (École Cantonale d'Art de Lausanne). He has exhibited his work in USA, Italy, France, Netherlands, Switzerland, Turkey, Hong Kong, Spain, and Mexico.

www.moises-hernandez.com
p170-173

Monitillo Marmi

Established in 1980 by Francesco Monitillo, Monitillo Marmi boasts a 12000sqm area in which stones, marbles, and granites are stored and processed. Monitillo Marmi is involved in several projects of construction sites and private residences, proposing a model based on the careful observation of details and tailor-made solutions. Monitillo's Pietre di Monitillo, a collection of design products for the home, has received a special mention in the ADI Design Index 2015 with the product Ovo.

www.monitillomarmi.it
p150-151, p216-217

nendo

Established by Oki Sato in 2002, nendo is a multi-disciplinary design agency based in Japan. Driven by the desire to create small "!" moments in daily life and overflowed with imagination, nendo has created a prolific amount of projects in architecture, interior, product, and graphic design. Their works have been displayed in various museums and galleries.

www.nendo.jp
p202-203, p208-209

Nolwenn Michea, Donia Ouertani, Flora Koel

Nolwenn Michea, Donia Ouertani, and Flora Koel are currently working on their Master degree in Product Design at the ESADSE (École Supérieure d'Art et Design de Saint-Etienne) in France.
nolwennmichea.com
florakoel.fr
cargocollective.com/DoniaOuertani
p214-215

Oddly Studio

Oddly, which means "unusual," is founded with the motivation to think and make things unique. In the process of separating and reorganizing the characteristics and roles of everyday objects, Oddly tends to create something that will bring new experience.
oddly-studio.com
p174-175, p218-219

Ohad Benit

Ohad Benit is an artist and designer specialized in conceptual art and design, ranging from product design, researching, developing, and producing projects in different fields. He deals with the seam line between art and design in order to stimulate a thorough discussion between the two approaches.
www.ohadbenit.com
p114-115

Pani Jurek

Pani Jurek was founded by Magda Jurek, an artist and designer. She graduated in painting at the Academy of Fine Arts in Warsaw and brings a conceptual approach to her work with an aim of creating products which are not obvious. She is also an advocate for sustainability.
www.panijurek.pl
p196-197, p199

Panter&Tourron

Panter&Tourron, founded by Stefano Panterotto and Alexis Tourron, is an independent design and consultancy studio based in Lausanne, Switzerland. They are specialized in performance products, spaces, identities, exhibitions, and events for companies and brands. Their vision challenges them to bring design outside its commonplaces, using simplicity as a luxury tool.
www.pantertourron.com
p158-159, p164-165

Pierre-Emmanuel Vandeputte

Pierre-Emmanuel Vandeputte is a Belgian designer who has graduated in Industrial Design from La Cambre in 2014. He opened his own studio in the same year in Brussels. His work is an enigmatic design that attempts to challenge the evidence, change the habits, and call for a new perception of reality.
www.pevdp.com
p032-033

Quentin de Coster

Born in Belgium in 1990, Quentin de Coster is an industrial designer specialized in product design, installation design, and creative direction. His work turns daily needs and gestures into thoughtful moments and experiences. Quentin regards design as an experience—a crossroads of function and aesthetic, logic and emotion.

His work is regularly exhibited around the world and has been featured by the likes of Design Milk, Azure, Dezeen, Designboom, etc.
www.quentindecoster.com
p207

Roxanne Flick

Roxanne Flick is an object designer from Luxembourg. She creates furniture and home accessories. She thinks that design has to offer more than shaping functional everyday objects—products are supposed to tell an own story. This interaction of concept and design is reflected in the development of her work.
www.roxanneflick.com
p190-191

Sam Linders

Graduated from the Design Academy Eindhoven, Sam Linders currently has the coolest job as a leather designer at ECCO LEATHER. He works fulltime and he is still learning a lot about leather, leather making, and of course working for a big company.
www.samlinders.com
p034-035

SHIFT

SHIFT is a design studio based in Monterrey, Mexico. They specialize in creating innovative and user-centered solutions in graphic, interior, product, and automotive design fields.
www.byshift.mx
p128-129, p156-157

Shinya Oguchi

Born in 1984, Shinya Oguchi graduated from Osaka University of Arts. After working for JDL, Lenovo Japan, and David Lewis Designers, he established an office in Tokyo in 2016. He has received many awards, like Red Dot Design Award Best of the Best, IF Design Award, etc.
www.shinyaoguchi.com
p092-093, p200

Shira Keret

Shira Keret is an Israeli product designer living and working in Tel Aviv.
www.shirakeret.com

Sitskie

Sitskie is a Detroit-based design studio and purveyor of fine crafted home goods. Sitskie was founded in 2012 by a husband-and-wife team, Vanessa and Adam Friedman. They proudly hand build all of their pieces locally.
www.sitskie.com

smarin

Smarin is a French design studio founded by Stéphanie Marin in 2003 in Nice. Smarin designs, develops and produces accessible and sustainable projects including textile, furniture, set design, and space planning. The cornerstone of the studio is to research and offer products made from natural and durable materials.
www.smarin.net

Sovrappensiero Design Studio

Sovrappensiero Design Studio was founded in Milan in 2007 by Lorenzo De Rosa and Ernesto Iadevaia. They collaborate with several companies such as Porada, Bialetti, Incipit, Corraini, WayPoint and Manerba. In 2014 they won the first prize in the competition "Young & Design" with their project "Cook" realized for the company Mamoli.
www.sovrappensiero.com

Studio Dessuant Bone

Established in 2014, Studio Dessuant Bone is a multi-disciplinary design consultancy based in Paris, specializing in direction, design, product and interiors. They pride themselves on creating projects that can traverse across a diverse range of clients and industries, including fashion, lifestyle, and creative product.
www.studiodessuantbone.com

Studio Lieven

Studio Lieven's main interest lies in re-imagining the nature and re-constructing it through human perceptual vehicles like geometry and science. Natural phenomena are the inspiration for Lieven's projects. Dividing nature and its phenomenon into bits and pieces and re-assembling them into understandable, usable, and relatable objects is the methodology of their work.
www.ninalieven.net

Studio Woojai

Studio Woojai is founded by WooJai Lee, a Korean-New Zealander designer based in Eindhoven, the Netherlands. Graduated from the Design Academy Eindhoven, he has great interest in working with materials to experiment and explore their hidden potentials. He also likes to draw and sculpt, and incorporate these qualities into his furniture designs.
www.woojai.com

SWNA

Established in 2008 by Sukwoo Lee, SWNA (formerly SWBK) is an industrial design studio located in Seoul, Korea. They are an incredibly passionate group of specialists who strive to create meaningful design for a better world.

They are not just a group of one-dimensional designers but rather three-dimensional thinkers, innovators, and ground breakers.
www.theswna.com

SY DESIGN

SY Design is a multi-awarded studio founded in Seoul in 2011. SY DESIGN engages in various fields such as furniture, product, space design, installation art, sculpture, and art direction. They do not consider an object simply as a tool but a media communicating with humans. Such unique design approach has been acknowledged in Korea as well as Asia and Europe.
www.sydesign.kr

Tianzhu Zhang

Tianzhu Zhang is an individual industrial designer who currently studies at RMIT University.
www.behance.net/xavierzhang

Tokujin Yoshioka

Active in the fields of design, contemporary art and architecture, Tokujin Yoshioka is highly acclaimed globally. He has designed for Issey Miyake and many global companies such as Cartier, Swarovski, Louis Vuitton, Hermès, and Toyota, and has been announcing new works at Salone del Mobile Milano. He has won many international awards and has been chosen by *Newsweek* magazine as one of the 100 Most Respected Japanese in the World.
www.tokujin.com

Vaidas Byla

Vaidas Byla is a young product designer from Lithuania.
www.behance.net/VBdizainas

Veega Design

Veega Design is a new brand based just outside London, specializing in handmade furniture, lighting and home accessories. It brings together a funky, bold, and contemporary aesthetic to a cozy home. Veega Design believes in the importance of thinking differently, seeing things from a new perceptions, enabling ideas to flourish, and most importantly creating comfortable living spaces.
www.veegadesign.com
p056-057

Virosh Rangalla

Virosh Rangalla is an industrial designer based in Toronto, Canada specialized in a number of fields including furniture design and consumer electronics. Whether it be physical products or digital experiences, his design philosophy focuses on creating functional and meaningful interactions and emphasizing intuitiveness and adaptability.
www.viroshrangalla.com
p010-011, p078-079

we+

Established in 2013 by Toshiya Hayashi and Hokuto Ando, we+ is a contemporary design studio based in Tokyo. Toshiya graduated from Hitotsubashi University in Tokyo and Hokuto graduated from Central Saint Martins in London. They develop their experimental approach to products, installations and graphics, by combining unconventional materials and technology to shift perspectives. Their works are presented by Gallery S. Bensimon in Paris and Spazio Rossana Orlandi in Milan.
weplus.jp
p182-183

Yaroslav Misonzhnikov

Yaroslav Misonzhnikov was born in 1988 in Saint Petersburg. He has obtained his Master degree in Spatial Design at Saint Petersburg State University in 2011. His work has been presented in famous exhibitions including SaloneSatellite, Salone del Mobile.
www.misonzhnikov.com
p212-213

Yenhao Chu

Yenhao Chu is a product designer born in Taiwan, whose father is a collector of Chinese antiques. She has been immersed in aesthetic environment since her childhood. After working as a product designer in Taipei, involving a variety of types of products, she is currently working on her master degree in ECAL, Switzerland. She has cooperated with Vitra, e15, and Victorinox during her study. She believes that a good design is like finding a balance between all the elements.
yenhaochu.com
p068, p069

Yonoh

Yonoh is a multidisciplinary creative studio set up by Clara del Portillo and Alex Selma in 2006. The studio is characterized by its simple yet functional designs. Simplicity, innovation and originality, without extravagance, are the backbone of their design philosophy. Versatility, timelessness, and adaptability are the cornerstones of the work done in their studio.
www.yonoh.es
p232

Yuhao Shen

Yu-Hao Shen is a Taiwanese product designer graduated from Institute of Applied Arts, National Chiao Tung University in Taiwan. In 2016, he participated in an exchange student program at Aalto University in Finland and worked as a product design intern in Teun Fleskens Studio based in the Netherlands.
cargocollective.com/shenyuhao
p038-039

YUUE

YUUE is an emerging design studio founded by Weng Xinyu and Tao Haiyue in 2015 in Berlin, Germany. YUUE works with visionary companies across the globe to create lighting, furniture, accessories and appliances, etc. Led by chef designer Weng Xinyu, YUUE lays great value on user experience and emotion. Its design approach combines traditional methods like modeling and crafting with digital tools like CAD and rapid prototyping.
www.yuuedesign.com
p112-113, p142-143, p198

ziinlife

Ziinlife discovers the hidden beauty from ordinary life and designs furniture with simple expression yet full of wonder and delight. They hope to make quality design furniture accessible and affordable. Ziinlife is a lovely surprise to be.
www.ziinlife.com
p074, p075

ACKNOWLEDGEMENTS

We would like to express our gratitude to all of the designers and companies for their generous contribution of images, ideas, and concepts. We are also very grateful to many other people whose names do not appear in the credits but who made specific contributions and provided support. Without them, the successful compilation of this book would not be possible. Special thanks to all of the contributors for sharing their innovation and creativity with all of our readers around the world. Our editorial team includes editors Jessie Tan, Chen Yaqin and book designer Chow Pakwah, to whom we are truly grateful.